OVERTHINKING

A STEP BY STEP GUIDE TO STOP WORRYING, TURN OFF YOUR THOUGHTS, STOP PROCRASTINATING AND INCREASE SELF-ESTEEM

RAY BENEDICT

© **Copyright 2020 - All rights reserved.**

The content contained within this book may not be reproduced, duplicated or transmitted without direct written permission from the author or the publisher.

Under no circumstances will any blame or legal responsibility be held against the publisher, or author, for any damages, reparation, or monetary loss due to the information contained within this book. Either directly or indirectly.

Legal Notice:

This book is copyright protected. This book is only for personal use. You cannot amend, distribute, sell, use, quote or paraphrase any part, or the content within this book, without the consent of the author or publisher.

Disclaimer Notice:

Please note the information contained within this document is for educational and entertainment purposes only. All effort has been executed to present accurate, up to date, and reliable, complete information. No warranties of any kind are declared or implied. Readers acknowledge that the author is not engaging in the rendering of legal, financial, medical or professional advice. The content within this book has been derived from various sources. Please consult a licensed professional before attempting any techniques outlined in this book.

By reading this document, the reader agrees that under no circumstances is the author responsible for any losses, direct or indirect, which are incurred as a result of the use of information contained within this document, including, but not limited to, — errors, omissions, or inaccuracies.

Tables of Contents

Introduction 4

Mental Clutter.. 18

Causes of Overthinking... 32

How To Achieve All Your Goals Finding Your Vocation 47

How To Stop Procrastinating And Change Habits....... 59

How To Stop Worrying And Increase Self-Esteem...... 74

How To Be More Positive (Step By Step Process)....... 91

Where Thoughts are Born And Why........................107

Change Habits..116

The Vicious Cycle Of Worrying 126

How to Make Important Decisions Today................142

Conclusion 153

Introduction

Many people suffer with overthinking on a daily basis without realizing that they are doing it, many people will make hundreds of 'to do' lists telling themselves that they are organized and being prepared. There is nothing wrong with this yet if you are the type to make lists for everything, ask yourself "are you following them?" Are you crossing things off your list and achieving them or are you simply making a list, which you then worry about doing and shortly afterwards make another list without every actually completing anything?

Overthinking can be debilitating, once it starts to hold you back and prevents you from doing the things you want to do then it becomes a problem. However once you realize you have an issue then you can do something about it.

Our brains are amazing yet being trapped inside our own can horrendous, our own personal hell. Nobody is more negative on ourselves than we are. Start using your overthinking in a positive way; instead of creating problems, try solving them. You can do this by making your to do list but also adding ways to do each item. For example, instead of just writing 'tidy the house' break it into bite size pieces such as 'clean the bath', 'sort out old clothes for the charity' and so on.

Another great tool is self-reflection. Many people mix this up with overthinking but self-reflection is healthy when it involves learning about yourself and takes into account both your strengths as well as your weaknesses. Self-reflection allows you to look at a situation in a different way in order to see things from another perspective. Overthinking on the other hand doesn't help you gain new insight or perspective because you are too busy dwelling on the negatives and often worrying about things out of your control.

If you are prone to overthinking then sometimes you just need to halt the mental chatter by switching your thoughts to something else. Mental strength exercises are good for this and there are many resources out there to instruct you in how to do this.

Switching tasks and carrying out a physical activity can be a great way to clear our minds. Some people find relaxing physical activity such as Yoga can empty their thoughts whilst others like something more strenuous like running. Sometimes even just getting up for a short walk can help so if you are stuck in a cycle of negativity and destructive thoughts try getting up and moving about.

This guide will focus on the following:

- What is overthinking
- Get rid of overthinking in 10 steps
- Overthinking is tied with depression
- How mindfulness can give you a new life
- Overthinking and procrastination... AND MORE!!!

What works for some doesn't work for other and sometimes what works for you one day doesn't work on another day. It really is about trial and error and sticking with it over time.

If you find your overthinking and anxiety is getting the better of you then turn to somebody. We can't always go it alone no matter how independent we want to be. If you have a friend or family member you feel comfortable with then go to them or if you would feel better speaking to somebody completely impartial then you may prefer to see a doctor or a mental health specialist who can help. Whatever you choose, remember there is no shame asking for help and nobody is judging you except you.

What is Overthinking?

There are many ways of describing overthinking. It can be understood as a situation where one cannot stop worrying and thinking about things. Overthinking is not a disorder. It involves a fear that grows in you and overwhelms you, but you can't help yourself but let it do so. In some cases, instead of crying it out, you simply opt to hold back your tears. It's the fear of failure: failing at your job, failing a certain class, failing in your relationships. Overthinking drives you to work hard for unrealistic expectations. This might sound productive, but in reality, you will be exhausted by maintaining this pace. Thinking too much leads to exhaustion. Emotionally and physically, you will feel exhausted since your mind never stops. It is always flooded with thoughts and the worst thing about it is that you believe there is nothing you can do.

Overthinking is that inner voice that tries to bring you down. It criticizes you and destroys your confidence and self-esteem. You not only doubt yourself, but you also doubt those who are close to you. It pushes you to second guess everything. Thinking too much can be compared to a spreading fire. It burns down everything that it finds on its way. Therefore, you will suffer as a result of overthinking.

Overthinking is when your mind clings to the faults that you have made and takes you through them throughout the day. When you overthink, your life will be on constant pause. You will always feel as though you are waiting for the right moment to do something. The problem is that this moment never arrives. You're always anticipating that something could go wrong. You will be overly careful when doing anything. This is influenced by the fact that you are just worried things might not work out as expected.

Signs that predict You Are an Overthinker

The following are clear indications that you think too much. You might try to deny it, but consider these signs and question yourself whether these are some of the things that you might have experienced.

You Overanalyze Everything

If you notice that you overanalyze everything around you, then you are certainly an overthinker. This means that you may try to find a deeper meaning in all the experiences that you go through. When meeting new people, instead of engaging in productive communication, you may focus instead on how other people perceive you. Someone could be giving you a particular look and you may make several assumptions just based on that look. Overthinking consumes you. You end up wasting a lot of energy trying to figure out and make sense of the world around you. What you don't realize is that not everything has intrinsic meaning.

You Think Too Much, But Don't Act

An overthinker will be affected by something called analysis paralysis. This is a scenario where you think too much about something, but don't do anything about it in the end. In this case, you spend a lot of time weighing the options you have at your disposal. At first, you make up your mind on what the best alternative might be. This means that you can't stop thinking about the possibilities and whether or not you made the right decision. Ultimately, you end up not making a decision. You only find yourself in a vicious circle where you simply think a lot, but there is little that you do. Perhaps the best strategy to prevent yourself from falling into a thinking trap is to try out the alternatives you have. A simple decision to act will make a huge difference.

You Can't Let Go

Often, we make erroneous decisions that could lead us to fail. When this happens, it can be daunting to let go more so when you reflect on the sacrifices you have made to get to the point you are at. You might feel that it is painful to let go after you have invested a lot of money on a certain business. The issue here is that you don't want to fail. However, it is important to realize that failing to let go only holds you back from trying out something else that could work. It also affects your life since you will think repeatedly about your failures. You need to move on. It's important that you shift your attention to something else instead of beating yourself up over something that is now out of your control. Convince yourself that there is nothing you can do about what has already happened apart from learning from it. The best thing you can do is to let go and move on.

You Always Want to Know Why

Without a doubt, the notion of asking why can be helpful to solve problems. This is because this probing attitude gets you the answers that you might be looking for. Nonetheless, it can also be damaging when you can't help but always wonder why. Normally, we are accustomed to answering questions from kids. They just love to ask why about anything and everything. They will not hesitate to ask you why you don't talk to your neighbor. Why children are born or simply why you love to walk. There's something unique about how children are curious. Overthinkers maintain such investigative attitude throughout their lives. As adults, there are certain things that only have surface meanings. Therefore, probing too much can only affect how other people see you.

You Analyze People

The way you see other people can also say a lot about you. In most cases, you get lost thinking too much about how other people behave. You may tend to judge everybody that you come across. This one walks in a funny way. That person is not dressed well. You wonder what someone sitting at the park is smiling about. When these thoughts fill your head, you will only drain yourself. Spending too much time focusing on other people will only deter you from using your mind productively. Instead of visualizing your goals and your future, you waste your energy mulling over little things that add no value to you.

Regular Insomnia

Do you find it hard to sleep sometimes? You may get worked up over the idea that your brain cannot shut down and stop thinking. Sadly, this can paralyze you since your brain doesn't get the rest that it deserves. Gradually, you will notice a decrease in your productivity. You are unlikely to feel good about yourself since there is little that you achieve. Worrying too much about not being able to sleep can make you uneasy and you may find yourself in a state of captivity. If this is something that you have been experiencing, then it sounds like you might be an overthinker. What could you do about this? First, if you are not active, then it is vital that you find a way of keeping yourself busy. In addition, meditation is a great practice that can help you stop overthinking and relax and focus on the present.

You Always Live in Fear

Are you afraid about what the future has in store for you? If you answer yes to this question, then chances are that you're caged in your mind. Living in fear could drive you to resort to drugs and alcohol as your best remedy.

You will gain the perception that by taking drugs, it will help you drown your sorrows and help you forget.

Unfortunately, this is not the case since drugs and alcohol are mere depressants. They slow down your brain functioning. As a result, you tend to believe that they are helping you forget.

You're Always Fatigued

Do you always wake up in the morning feeling tired? This could be a result of stress or depression. Instead of living a productive life, you find yourself waking up late, tired, and unmotivated. The reason why this happens is because you don't give your mind an opportunity to rest. It has been working day and night. In the evening, instead of sleeping you find yourself awake all night because you are overthinking. Your mind cannot work for 24 hours straight at the same level of functioning. You will only suffer from burnouts. You need to give your mind ample time to rest and reboot.

You Don't Live in the Present

Do you find it difficult to enjoy life? Why do you think you find it daunting to sit back, relax, and be happy with your friends? The mere fact that you can't stay in the present implies that you won't focus on what is happening in the present. Overthinking will blind you from noticing anything good that is currently happening around you.

You will often think about the worst that can happen. The issue is that you are trapped in your mind and there is nothing outside your thoughts that you can constructively think about.

Failure to live in the present denies you the opportunity to improve relationships with other people. In fact, you will live in fear that they will criticize you. Therefore, you will only want to exist in your cocoon. Again, this will lead to stress.

Types of Overthinking

Abstract Thinking

This refers to a form of thinking which goes beyond concrete realities. For instance, when you are trying to formulate theories to explain your observations, then you're engaging in abstract thinking. When your business is not performing well, you might jump to the conclusion that it's because of the economy.

Complexity

The complexity form of overthinking comes about when there are many factors to consider in your decision-making process. In this case, these numerous factors could prevent you from weighing the true importance of each one of them. The effect is that it could prevent you from making decisions promptly.

Avoidance

Avoidance occurs when one tries to avoid doing something by using the decision-making process as their excuse.

Cold Logic

When using cold logic to think, you tend to avoid relying on human factors, including language, culture, personality, emotion, and social dynamics. The outcome is that you end up making biased decisions that do not consider legal or social realities.

Intuition Neglect

This occurs when one fails to consider what they already know. In other words, one opts to overthink something that they already know a thing or two about. Instead of following your gut instinct, you overthink and end up making the wrong decisions.

Creating Problems

You may also find yourself thinking in a way where you are creating problems that are not there in the first place. There are certain situations or things which are not as complex as you think. In ordinary situations, it would have taken you a minute or two to solve them. It is vital to focus more on the bigger picture and not nitpick at the details. Sometimes it is important to see things as they are. Don't complicate your life by thinking of potential problems.

Magnifying the Issue

Usually, small problems require simple solutions. There are instances where we amplify these problems and we end up coming up with overly complex solutions to solve them. This is another form of overthinking. You end up wasting your resources to come up with huge solutions that don't match the problems you are experiencing.

Fear of Failure

Fear of failure is not a new concept to most people. In fact, this is what motivates most of us to work hard. Instead of working hard for a bright future, you find yourself drawing motivation from the fear you have developed inside you.

Irrelevant Decisions

There are times when we make irrelevant decisions because we force ourselves to make these decisions, yet we are not required to make them. For instance, when thinking about our future, there are instances where we end up making irrelevant decisions based on assumptions.

Getting married, for example, based on the assumptions you have, you might conclude that you need to get married because you're getting old.

Mental Clutter

Your home is not the only thing that is susceptible to clutter. In fact, a cluttered mind and a cluttered home are one and the same. For example, holding onto clutter is the same as holding onto the past. You have it hard to let go of some items, even when you know you should, because of the sentimental value and the memories which are attached to it. Sometimes you don't even want to get rid of it because it was a gift and you're worried about hurting the other person's feelings. You know you're never going to use it, but you hold onto it anyway. Holding onto items that are no longer of any use to you will stop you from moving forward because you can't look ahead when you're constantly looking back. It's the same thing when your mind is cluttered. You hold onto the past because you can't bring yourself to let go, you keep having the same thoughts over and over again, and you have a hard time letting go of certain memories that hurt, even when you know that you should.

Understanding physical clutter is a lot easier than understanding mental clutter. With physical clutter, we can see it. We know clutter is referring to the piles and stacks of unnecessary items we have around the home. Mental clutter is a little harder to define. Have you ever had days when you feel so frazzled? Like your mind is being pulled in a million different directions and you feel exhausted from the sheer energy you've had to expand thinking and processing the thoughts you have? On any given day, the average person has about 60,000 to 80,000 thoughts running through our minds. That's approximately 2,500 to 3,300 thought that you're churning out in an hour. Other experts believe that number may be slightly smaller, an average of 50,000 thoughts a day perhaps. That's still a big number, and what's worse, more than half of the thoughts you have are not beneficial. Most of the thought are either useless, or they are unimportant, which means they are taking up all that space in your mind of nothing.

Our brain is active and constantly on the move, like a butterfly flitting from one beautiful flower to the next, never stopping to stand still long enough. Thinking is such an automatic process that we don't realize the thoughts that we're having unless it is something significant that grabs our attention. We're completely oblivious to how these thoughts are taking up too much space in our mind, making it difficult to focus and concentrate, nothing but a distraction, taking your attention away from what you should be focusing on in your life instead. The time and the hours that you spend thinking unnecessary thoughts could be put to better use doing something productive, something that is going to bring you one step closer to your goals. A cluttered mind distracts you from what's important in life, taking up more of your attention and time than it should.

What is a cluttered mind? It is a mind that:

- Has a confusing thought process

- Can't operate in a calm, productive, and focused manner

- That struggles to stay positive

- That struggles to hold on to happiness

- That is full of thoughts that don't contribute in a positive way to your life or wellbeing

- Is lacking direction

- Ruminates too much

- Obsesses about what is beyond your control

- Has a hard time letting go of negativity,

resentment, and anger

- Can be easily swayed by circumstances, opinions, and criticism

- Easily distracted by external circumstances

In short, a cluttered mind results in a negative mindset. The most dangerous thing about a cluttered mindset is that you're relinquishing control. You're giving up control of your life by letting your thoughts dictate what you should think and how you should feel. You forget that you are the one with the power to control your life, not your mind and certainly not your thoughts. When you give up and leave it to your thoughts to decide your fate, when you no longer take responsibility for your thoughts and actions, that's a clear sign that something needs to change if you want to initiate any kind of change in your life for the better.

How Clutter Affects the Brain

If your brain were a computer, clutter would represent having too many tabs open in the brain at one time. It's messy, disorganized, and makes it hard to focus on anything.

Because there are so many thoughts that are taking

place in our mind at any given time, when these thoughts are negative or contradict each other, they start to cause problems. These thoughts are partially responsible for the stress, anxiety, and depression that so many people are battling with today, not realizing how mental clutter has a part to play in it. When your thoughts begin affecting you in a very negative way, it's a real problem. Harboring negative emotions is a sign that your mind is cluttered. It starts with one thought, one feeling and before you know it, you're sliding down a very slippery slope of unhappy emotions and you don't know how to slow down anymore. Negativity puts your mind in a bad place you never want it to be in, and it can quickly strip you of any possibility of happiness.

Your brain is not designed to have its attention pulled in so many different directions. Your brain needs to be organized. At peace. Focused on one thing at a time, preferably something positive and uplifting that makes you feel good. The trouble is, negativity is not entirely avoidable. There will be some moments in life that are less than pleasant. It's even worse when we lack the ability to properly organize and filter the information that we receive. Like your email inbox. If you don't delete or filter the important emails from the junk mail, everything is just going to pile together in one big mess, making your inbox too stressful to look at or even deal with. To say we're never going to feel the stressful effects of negativity would be a lie. We can't always avoid them, but what you can do is learn how to process these those, assess them, and deal with them in better, healthier ways so they don't linger and clutter your mind.

Your mental habits are the reason you're not reaching your full potential. Your "busy" mind is the reason you feel "stuck", stressed, anxious and overwhelmed so easily. Clutter is bad for your brain and the negativity it causes is one of the most debilitating hindrances you can have, taking up more than its fair share of space in your mind that there is no room for anything else. Don't forget about the physical clutter that is secretly affecting you in the background too without you knowing it. There's a saying that goes: "Mess equals stress" and there's a very good reason why. Being surrounded by disorganization makes it hard for anyone to concentrate. We are so conditioned to a life of materialism that we genuinely believe the decisions about the purchases we make are based on careful thought and sound logic. We make excuses and give reasons as to why we need to purchase more stuff. We make purchases in the hopes that we will finally become a happier version of ourselves, but when that doesn't happen, we become unhappy and the emotions we feel only aggravate the mental clutter that is already there.

What Decluttering Is NOT

Decluttering is not just necessary, it's satisfying. To feel like an immense weight has been lifted off your mind is liberating. Your mind is not an abandoned attic. It's not a place you can come and dump your thoughts, hoping they will either go away on their own or that you'll forget about them. The emotions, dreams, goals, unfulfilled desires, past memories are all still going to be there, and they'll continue to be there until you find a way to properly process and organize the thoughts you have. When you spring clean your home, doesn't it make you feel good to toss out all that unnecessary junk? That's the same thing you need to do with your mind. Toss out all the unnecessary and organize what remains.

Mental Decluttering Is: Confronting Your Feelings

Sweeping them under the rug is not going to work. That strategy has never worked, and it never will. Avoidance and denial are two coping mechanisms you need to leave behind because trying to conceal your emotions is only going to lead to emotional and mental fatigue. The thought of confronting your unpleasant emotions sounds dreadful, but it is a necessary part of the decluttering process. Suppressing your emotions prevents your brain from doing a good job of thinking clearly.

Mental Decluttering Is Not: Avoiding Worry Altogether

Like negativity, worry is not something you can avoid entirely. There will be moments where you are bound to worry, it's an inevitable part of life. Mental decluttering is not about running away or trying to deny and block out worry altogether, but to try and be more proactive about it. Instead of letting the worry take over your entire day, keep your mind organized by allowing yourself time to worry before you return to your other tasks. In between tasks, pick a time that works best, and schedule 5 to 10 minutes specifically for your worries.

There is always going to be something to worry about. You can't avoid worry forever, so what you're doing to do instead is to be more proactive about it. Instead of letting the worry take over your entire day, keep your mind organized by allowing yourself time to worry before you return to your other tasks. Rehash your concerns, but think about solutions instead of distorting those thoughts and making yourself feel worse. Train your brain to be solution-oriented instead of circling over the same worry repeatedly. This keeps the worries from spinning out of control and distracting you throughout the day so you can still stay on top of everything you need to do and process your worries without neglecting them.

Mental Decluttering Is: Tidying Up Your Environment

The environment you spend the most time in is going to have the biggest influence on your psyche. It's not a good thing that we have that become so used to our environment being noisy, hectic, stressful, and messy that we don't even notice it anymore. There's a good chance at least one area (if not several) of your home that is cluttered with far too much stuff.

How did it get to such an extent? Well, for one thing, most of us are far too busy these days, rushing from one appointment to the next. We spend long days at the office and by the time we get home, we're too exhausted to do anything else. Another thing is that cleaning is not exactly an activity many look forward to, and when you procrastinate and keep putting off cleaning the mess around your home, that's how clutter starts to build. The bigger the mess, the longer it is going to take you to clean. A 5-minute cleanup is now going to take 2-3 hours to get done when the mess has grown far too big. Both your home and your mind are like a boat on the ocean. Keep pilling clutter in that boat it will eventually sink to the bottom under the weight of it all.

Mental Decluttering Is Not: Limited to Materialistic Possessions

Decluttering is not limited to removing the excess physical items around your home. In fact, mental decluttering encompasses all aspects of your life. Everything that we're exposed to, everything we do, everything we say or think affects the brain in one way or another. Mental decluttering is also about eliminating toxic relationships, old ideas, and bad habits. Anything in your environment that is negative needs to be eliminated. This includes any toxic individuals who happen to be in your life.

Can Decluttering Change Your Life?

It's hard to make a fresh start when your old worries still maintain their hold on you. Every new year, most people begin with a list of new year resolutions enthusiastically prepared. Motivations run high and we all intend to keep see these resolutions through in the end. But as the year goes on, the initial excitement slowly wanes and we find ourselves slipping back into old habits. Slowly, the lack of motivation begins creeping into the other areas of your life. You find it hard to get anything done, productivity is running low, you're easily distracted, you feel tired all the time, you've lost your sense of purpose and thoughts of the past still haunt you. Without decluttering your mind, you'll be trapped in this toxic cycle of thought forever, wasting several good years of your life feeling unhappy.

Decluttering mentally (and physically) is going to change your life. Clutter is unnecessary work, and unnecessary work only leads to stress. It's a burden to take on more than you can handle, and when the mess gets so bad you feel overwhelmed, there's only one thing left to do. Free yourself. Clutter is distracting and annoying, causing far too much negativity that we don't need. Instead of agonizing, it's time to start organizing. Besides the obvious benefit of having a cleaner environment and a happier mind, decluttering is the solution you've been looking for and this is why it's going to benefit your life:

- More Room for What Matters - Purging the unnecessary out of your life, both physical and mental, you're creating space. That space makes you feel like you can breathe again. Accumulating physical items makes it even harder for us to let go and we hold on to things sometimes not because of the memory attached to it but because we always think "What if I need this tomorrow or next week or next year?". Be honest though, how many times have you actually needed the items you're holding on to "just in case"? You already have everything you need to survive and be happy, and those are the items you use daily. If you're not using it regularly, you don't need it.

• A Greater Sense of Happiness - With a better focus on what's important in life, mental and physical decluttering also brings you joy because you have a better focus on things that matter. You're more efficient, concentrate better, and you know what your priorities are. You find yourself enjoying life because you're now free from what was making you unhappy in the past.

• Peace of Mind - A noisy mind is one that can never be at peace. How could you be when your thoughts are either making you anxious or worried or both. We create a lot of stress for ourselves and the attachment to materialism certainly doesn't help matters either. Buying more stuff doesn't make us happy. Maybe it does at the time of purchase, but that feeling soon fades away. Materialism is nothing more than trying to fill an empty void we don't want to deal with, and once you start embracing this reality, it's easier to let go of everything that weighs you down.

- It Changes the Way You Think – It's hard to ever truly feel happy if you continue to anchor your happiness to external possessions. Decluttering your mind changes the way that you think, and you begin to find happiness from within instead of relying on materialism and frivolous world possessions that never last for long. When there are fewer distractions in your life, you will be able to shift your focus on what truly matters in your life. For example, your health, your well-being, your family, your friends, your partner, your spouse, your pets, your hobbies, your passion, and all the other things will start to take precedence once again in your life and these are the things that you should be valuing more than how many shiny new object or clothes you were able to purchase.

- Greater Efficiency - Suddenly, with a lot less stuff in your life you find yourself becoming a lot more efficient than what you were before. You can concentrate better, your priorities more in focus, you find yourself feeling lighter, happier, and able to work a lot more efficiently and make more productive use of your time because you have less things around you that distract you. You will find yourself managing your time more efficiently with less distractions, and you won't feel as pressure as you once did before because of this. You will be able to accomplish more, feel more productive, and you won't feel as pressed for time as you once did because there is nothing that is distracting you from what you should be doing.

- Setting an Example for Future Generations - Whether you have kids right now or in the future, you'll be setting a good example when you live a simple, clutter-free, uncomplicated life. You'll be teaching them valuable life lessons, to see that material possessions are not responsible for bringing you happiness, and to be happy and grateful for the things which they already possess in their lives. It helps them to value what they have more, and learn to distinguish between needs and wants.

Causes of Overthinking

There is a high possibility of experiencing somatopsychological problems if your vagus nerve is inflamed or damaged. These problems are mostly related to your psychological aspect and can only be noticed through your actions, and they initiated in your head as it depends on how your brain responds to different situations, so you need to understand the two systems of the vagus nerve continuously communicate with the brain, mainly about other body organs. The sympathetic nervous system is responsible for keeping you in action by feeding the cortisol and the adrenaline while the parasympathetic nervous system is reliable while you are relaxed or resting.

In other words, the sympathetic system activates actions while the parasympathetic decelerates actions and keeps you at rest. However, the latter utilizes acetylcholine as neurotransmitters that control the blood pressure and the heart rate to create a perfect condition for relaxation. As a part of the body's autonomous nervous system, the vagus nerve may fail or experience damage hindering its full potential to the body. The most common condition that affects the vagal nerve is inflammation that makes it malfunction. This condition could worsen the functioning of the whole body as the vagal nerve facilitates essential processes that keep the body healthy and kicking.

Chronic stress

The problem is associated with overthinking things that might be beyond your control. Stress can also be a result of issues in your vagal nerve. For instance, when your body is exposed to harmful situations, it releases chemicals that are meant to respond appropriately and avoid injury. As noted before, the sympathetic nervous system stimulates the response through the fight-or-flight reaction, and it is at this time that your heart rate increases to quickly supply blood to the rushing body parts and muscles. The response likewise enhances the quickened inhalation of oxygen to assist in blood oxygenation. In this case, stress acts as a protective mechanism that your body initiates to keep you alert and out of danger.

There are different perceptions of stress among people. In other words, what causes stress for one person might be of little concern to the other, and people have different ways and potential to deal with it. This means that if stress is meant to prevent you from danger, then it should not be treated as a bad thing. Besides, our bodies have a unique mechanism that is intended to deal with specific doses of stress. However, the body's capabilities could weaken as you may be overwhelmed by chronic stress that could be as a result of vagal nerve inflammation or damage. This type of stress impacts almost every aspect of your life, including physical health and emotions. The chronic stress is also characterized by low esteem where you feel worthless and not comfortable while in public.

If you are suffering from chronic stress, you are likely to feel overwhelmed and easily agitated by others. As a result, you end up avoiding interactions with your peers as you feel they want to control you. Avoiding people and having low self-esteem makes you suffer in isolation as you may not realize the seriousness of the condition. With this in mind, the emotional symptoms of chronic stress could end up being a serious condition if not detected and treated. Consequently, your judgment becomes impaired by the condition as you get prone to the inability to focus and forgetfulness. You also remain pessimistic and unable to view your life positively and exhibit nervousness through behaviors such as fidgeting and nail-biting.

First, people with chronic stress seem to avoid complex responsibilities. They also experience sudden changes in your appetite where they either eat excessively or not eat at all. Second, procrastination is also associated with chronic stress, and you could be at risk of indulging in alcohol and drug abuse. Therefore, you should ask for feedback if you think that you are suffering from stress. A doctor will usually record the observations and what you report to come to a proper conclusion about the condition you are suffering from. In this case, the underlying cause of chronic stress is a dysfunctional vagus nerve, so you should take the necessary measures to ensure that you start vagal verve treatment to normalize its functionality.

Anxiety and Panic Attacks

Whenever you come across a stressful situation, the body activates the sympathetic nervous system of the vagus nerve. In most cases, the system is reversed once the situation is over. However, the persistence of the tension would mean that the sensitive effect of the vagus nerve would be prolonged until you are out of harm's way. The effect is usually triggered and ended by a physiological response in your body, but a prolonged fight-or-flight response would cause problems for your body. The situation would lead to the activation of the intestine and the adrenal axis of the brain. As a result, the brain increases the production of hormones that travel through the bloodstream to stimulate the adrenaline and cortisol induction.

The hormones act as inflammatory precursors and immune suppressors, causing the anxiety that could make you ill and depressed, so the chronic anxiety increases the production of glutamate in the brain, which, when combined with cortisol, reduces the hippocampus in charge of memory retention. The worsening of this situation leads to the development of anxiety disorder characterized by panic attacks. The problem is characterized by a sense that you are in an impending danger or your life is at risk. These false signs may be frequent, depending on the seriousness of the condition. With this condition, you feel afraid of losing your valuables or as if you are about to die. In most cases, the effect seems uncontrollable as the panic creates an illusion that it has been decided elsewhere.

At this time, your heart rate is increased due to the tension, making it pound on your chest as your breath goes wild. The blood pressure increases as the body take it as an attack. These panic attacks might confuse your body as they give false alarms making your body sweat as if you are in a serious situation even though you may be lying on your couch. The helplessness associated with anxiety and panic attacks leaves you trembling with fear of imagined imminent danger, and you will realize that your body is shaking uncontrollably due to a perceived situation.

The quickened breathing associated with anxiety makes your throat experience fast air movement as the lungs try to suck as much air as possible to supply to the heart, resulting to experience tightness in your throat and a burning effect. You may also fall short of breath as the heart rate increases, as well as experience prolonged chills if you suffer from anxiety and panic attacks. These chills could be against the sweating and heat produced by the body as your adrenaline keeps you in the fight-or-flight reaction. This problem makes you look confused and unaware of the immediate environment.

The condition should be taken seriously as it could lead to suicidal thoughts and actions as the victim sees no other way out. This is because the experiences in the body are severe and complicated and would require immediate treatment to avoid causing accidents and incidents. The hot rashes experienced in this problem are experienced in the neck, chest, or stomach and are indications that the body is at the full alert of the faced danger. Generally, these illusions make the person feel detached from the real world and it would be hard to communicate with them when under panic attacks. In other words, their mind takes them to the world where they see a danger in every corner. The total panic is so real that the person continually experiences a tingling and numb sensation.

Other characteristics of anxiety and panic attacks include headache, chest pain, and dizziness, especially after the attack is over. During this time, the victim relaxes and tries to recover lost energy, but with chronic panic attacks, the victim keeps on worrying that the experience may happen again. They also feel uncomfortable associating with others and attending public functions as they are wary of possible attacks. At this time, the body exerts these symptoms due to the confusion caused by the dysfunctional vagus nerve, so if you experience these symptoms, you should see a doctor check on the condition of your vagus nerve and take the necessary measures.

Phobias

Vagal inflammation is known to cause phobias as one of the somatopsychological problems in the human body. Mostly, the problem is characterized by a deep sense of panic and irrational fear reaction. When you are in this condition, you encounter different sources of fear, depending on how you perceive the environment. In some instances, you could be experiencing phobia in specific situations, objects, or places. This form of vagal nerve damage is known to complicate how your brain interprets some aspects of the environment, so you end up feeling insecure in dark or quiet environments, especially if you have had a frightening experience before.

The effects of phobia vary depending on the seriousness as well as the body's mechanism to repair damaged tissues. These conditions determine the impact of phobia in your body as it could only be an annoying experience or build up to a severe and disabling. If you experience phobia, you might be helpless about it as it is caused by other underlying conditions such as vagal nerve inflammation. Therefore, you are prone to stress as you always remain afraid of a possible attack, making you unproductive and unsocial, especially in the workplace. The condition may be different from one person to the other, hence the different categorization according to the trigger and symptoms.

One common type of the condition is known as agro phobia which is characterized by the panic of situations and places that you cannot escape from. Mostly, people who have an agro phobia are afraid of being in open places such as outside their houses or in crowded places. People feel uncomfortable while in social areas and like to stay most of their time indoors. The main reason why these people avoid public places is due to the anxiety of experiencing phobia publicly, which might embarrass them and leave them helpless. In some cases, people with an agro phobia may experience a health emergency, making them remain in places where they could ask for an urgent response.

Social phobia has relatively similar characteristics and is also known as social anxiety disorder when combined with symptoms of anxiety. As the name suggests, the victims of this disorder avoid social places and prefer staying in isolation for fear of humiliation and discrimination in case they become phobic. This type of phobia is so serious as it could be caused by a simple interaction such as answering a phone call or talking to a stranger. It makes the victims go out of their way to avoid these interactions making life hard for them, especially if they are working or attending school. A phobia may be triggered by a specific object with common categories being the environment, medical, situations, or animals.

In this case, you experience phobia after experiencing environmental conditions such as storm or lightning, while an animal phobia is as a result of encountering animals such as rodents or snakes. In medical phobia, you feel threatened by the sight of blood or syringe. These experiences are hard to live with, and you should take the necessary steps to ensure that the condition is controlled to help you live happily and fearlessly. The problem is characterized by uncontrollable anxiety, especially when you experience a source of fear. Also, you may find yourself doing extra lengths to ensure that you avoid perceived sources of concern even if it means changing direction. If you are affected by this problem, you are likely to be unproductive in your workplace as you could not function properly when the source of fear is around.

It will be hard to control the feeling even after you realize that the fear is exaggerated, unreasonable, and irrational. Some of the physical effects of phobia include trembling and abnormal breathing. At this time, the body is accelerating the supply of blood and chemicals to the body to tackle the perceived threat, and there is confusion and disorientation as you remain stuck between understanding the danger and taking swift action to get out of danger. The accelerated heartbeats are likely to cause abnormal breathing which could lead to pain in the chest as the lungs try to grasp as much oxygen as they can. The best remedy for this condition would be to understand the underlying cause and seek medical help to repair and heal the damaged vagus nerve.

Bipolar disorder

The problem is also caused by vagal dysfunction and inflammation and was formerly referred to as a manic depression. It is a mental condition that triggers a moody feeling and swinging emotions. When the emotions are high, they are referred to as mania or hypomania, and depression when they are low. If you are depressed, you probably will experience hopelessness, sadness, and lost pleasure and interest. The feeling makes you hate activities that you liked before and lose interest in meeting the people you love. However, the feeling is sometimes short-lived as you may suddenly experience high moods that make you feel euphoric and irritably full of energy.

The drastic changes in mood significantly affect how you behave, judge, or sleep. It also hinders you from clear reasoning and making the right decision. There are numerous episodes of these mood swings that occur several times annually. In some cases, you may experience changes in events and emotional symptoms, while others may not experience them at all. The condition is manageable through the follow up of a treatment plan that includes counseling and medication. When a dysfunctional vagus nerve causes the condition, it could only be treated by healing the nerve. Several types of this disorder include depression and hypomania. These symptoms could cause drastic life effects and significant distress if left unaddressed.

Bipolar disorder is experienced when the condition triggers a break from reality and makes you fear your imagination. It is characterized by a single manic episode and occurs either before or after the incident. Bipolar II is characterized by a major depressive episode that lasts for weeks followed by a hypomanic episode that happens for about a week. The condition is more common in women but is also experienced by men. In cyclothymia, you experience bouts of depression and hypomania, which are relatively shorter than those caused by the last two types. Additionally, the condition is characterized by a month or two for stability when the problem recurs and extends for some weeks. The mania and hypomania episodes are distinct in their symptoms, but the mania episode is more severe and is known to cause problems in public places such as workplaces or schools.

The condition also affects your relationship with your peers and family as it distances you from the reality hence the need to take drastic measures to curb it. The mania and hypomania episodes are characterized by jumpy and abnormal upbeats where you remain restless and agitated by things that might be perceived or out of control. The condition increases your activities as you seem to have extra energy to perform various tasks. These episodes make you feel overconfident and a sense of well-being, assuring you that you can succeed in everything you try and that you are perfect. The euphoria could lead to embarrassment as you try to prove your point. You run out of control in whatever you do as you seem to take over the management in your company or want to replace the monitor in your class.

You may always remain and uncontrollably talkative and seem excited about topics that could be boring to your audience. Bipolar disorder keeps your body engaged, hence the talkativeness and overreaction to minor things. Your thoughts also remain at a high rate as they think about things that could be out of the world. The increased interest in uncommon things could make you lose interest and easily diverted to other topics, so you quickly lose interest and remain unpredictable on the issues that you would address. The major depressive episodes cause noticeable difficulties in your daily activities with most of the symptoms being psychological. The effects could make you lose or gain weight as you suffer from swing appetite. The feeling of worthlessness associated with this disorder could lead to inappropriate guilt. If you suffer from this condition, you are likely to have difficulties thinking or concentrating with a high possibility of developing suicidal thoughts. For that reason, you should understand the underlying cause of the condition and take drastic measures to address it.

With the healing of the vagal nerve, you are sure to regain your consciousness and suppress the disorder.

How To Achieve All Your Goals Finding Your Vocation

A mind that is cluttered is indecisive, unproductive, and stuck in its way. It is necessary to get rid of this clutter, just as much as you would do to your physical clutter, as it helps you to concentrate on your goals and make way for things you deem essential. Below is a three-step process that will help you to get rid of any mental clutter that can prevent you from achieving your goals.

1. Be Decisive

When you know what you want, achieving your set goals becomes easier to achieve than most people think. Every day, we face a plethora of problems that demand that we make decisions that will get us closer to our goals or farther from them. What should be the agenda for next week's meeting? Should I register for that course? What should I write in that e-mail? When should I approach that investor? What should I do about my marriage?

You have so much on your mind, and making a decision seems like something too enormous, but the more you delay in making that decision, the more you find it challenging to achieve your goals. According to numerous researchers, "the reason why most people are not decisive in making decisions that will drive them towards their goals, is not that they do not know the right decision to take, but due to the fear of making the wrong one."

Being decisive is one vital way to declutter your mind. So, stop worrying and start taking the right steps. Evaluate the pros and cons of every choice that you have and make the right step without looking back.

Prioritize

Make your goals clearer and make a to-do list of what you want to do each day/week/month and if possible, each year, this is the best way to become decisive about your goals.

You need to figure out the goals that matter most to you; this should be your life ambitions and long-term goals. Make a list of those priorities you deem important and create an action plan that will help you to achieve your life goals.

Let Go

It is crucial to consciously let go of all negative thinking and emotions that can weigh you down. Negative emotions can make you have an anxiety disorder and can lead to chronic stress.

One way to let go is by talking to a support system about how you feel about your goals, which can help you to reason clearly and give you another perspective.

Become aware of your thoughts, monitor those thoughts regularly, and be ready to get rid of those thoughts that do not serve you.

7.2. Programs that can help you to declutter your mind

7.2.1. Cognitive Behavioural Therapy

This program focuses on exploring the relationships around your feelings, behaviours, and thoughts.

During Cognitive Behavioural Therapy, a therapist will carefully walk you through your mind to uncover negative thought patterns and how they may be causing harm to you by being the source of your self-destructive beliefs and behaviors.

By addressing these negative thought patterns, you and your therapist can come up with new thought patterns that are healthier and would help you to produce healthier beliefs and behaviors. For example, if you have thoughts of low esteem (I am a failure, I can't get anything done), CBT can help you replace it with (I can do this most of the time, I may not get it right at first, but I can always try again).

Often, your therapist will give you homework between sessions where you practice replacing your negative thought with thoughts that are more realistic and positive, or your therapist can ask you to record your negative thoughts in a journal.

CBT is useful in treating anxiety disorders, bipolar disorder, schizophrenia, eating disorders, depression, and stress.

7.2.2. Exposure Therapy

This type of cognitive-behavioral therapy is mostly used to treat post-traumatic stress, obsessive-compulsive disorder, and phobias. During this therapy, your therapist will work with you to identify what triggers your anxiety and will teach you techniques to avoid the triggers or avoid reacting to those triggers. This therapy helps you to confront what triggers your concerns in a safe environment.

Two methods can be used to perform exposure therapy.

One presents a small amount of triggering stimulus and escalates them overtime while the other gives a considerably large amount of the triggering stimulus all at once. Both methods will help you to cope with what triggers your anxiety, stress, worry, etc.

7.2.3. Psychodynamic Psychotherapy

This program helps you to recognize negative thinking and habits that are due to past experiences and helps you to resolve them. This type of therapy makes use of free association and open-ended questions so that you can have the opportunity to discuss whatever you have on your mind. The therapist will then work with you to unconscious patterns of negative thoughts and emotions and how they may be as a result of past experiences. By bringing you to the understanding that it was your past experiences that led to your present condition, your therapist can then guide you on how to overcome unhelpful feelings and behaviors.

7.2.4. Therapy Pets

If you spend time with domestic animals, it can reduce your symptoms of depression, stress, anxiety, pain, and fatigue. Nursing homes, hospitals, and other medical facilities are known to sometimes make use of this therapy by making use of pet animals.

Research has shown that if you spend time with pets, it can reduce your level of anxiety more than a lot of popular recreational activities. They are particularly helpful for children and veterans with PTSD.

7.3. How to Develop Self-Esteem

How you feel about yourself is very important to your happiness in life. Having a high opinion of yourself, what you do, who you are and love for yourself is one important thing that people have little of in today's society.

Some benefits of developing high self-esteem include;

-   Life becomes lighter and more straightforward.

-   More inner stability.

-   Less self-sabotage.

-   You'll be a more admirable person to your close ones and colleagues at work.

-   You'll be happier.

Those are the benefit of developing good self-esteem, but how do you develop this habit? Here's how;

1. Say "Stop" to your inner critic

An excellent place to start if you want to raise your self-esteem is by learning how to replace the voice of your inner critic.

Everyone has an inner critic that often spurs us to do things to gain the acceptance of others in your life and on social media. This need to gain acceptance drags your self-esteem down as you will begin to judge yourself by how others judge you.

The inner critic is that voice inside our head that says destructive thought in your mind. For example, it says words like;

- You are not worthy of this position; it's above your technical skills.

- You aren't worthy of that girl; she will leave you for another.

- You are a bad mother.

You don't have to accept the things the inner critic says to you; there are ways to minimize them and replace this thought with more positive thinking. You can change what you think about yourself.

One way to get over the inner-critic is by stopping whatever the inner critic pipes up in your mind is to create a stop-word or stop-phrase for it.

Once the inner critic brings a thought to you, shout "Stop" in your mind. Or come up with your word or phrase that can stop the train of thought. Then refocus your thoughts to more positive things.

2. Use healthier motivational habits

To reduce the inner critic's intensity, motivate yourself to raise your self-esteem, and take positive actions.

3. Take a break for self-appreciation

Self-appreciation is very fun and straightforward, and you will notice a remarkable difference if you spend just two minutes on it every day of the month. Here's how to go about it;

Slowly take a deep breath and ask yourself this question "What are the three things I like about my life?" A few examples of answers you can give yourself are;

- What I write impacts a lot of people.

- I'm a good boss at work.

- I'm very caring and thoughtful when it comes to dogs.

These talks won't just help you build your self-esteem;

they will also turn negative moods into a good one.

4. Do the right thing.

You will raise and strengthen your self-esteem when you do what you think is right. It might be a small thing like going to the gym in the morning or helping your child with their studies.

To make it more effective, stay consistent in the right thing you've made up your mind to do. Make sure you take action every day.

5. Handle mistakes and failures positively

It is normal to stumble and fall if you go outside of your comfort zone. It is necessary if you want to do things that matter in life. Everyone that has got to great heights in life did; you hardly hear them talk about it. So, remember that, and when you falter try to do these things;

- Be your best friend: Rather than beating yourself up and being angry about it, ask yourself this question. Who will support me in this situation? How will the person help me? Then start imagining the person advising you.

- Find the upside: one other way to be more constructive is to focus more on opportunities and optimism. Ask yourself these questions: What can I learn from this? What benefit can I derive from this situation? These will help you to change your viewpoint on failure.

7.4. How to Develop the New You

A lot of us build up images in our heads about who we are "I'm boring, I'm suffering from depression," etc. we reiterate this point to ourselves, and we convince our mind that it's the way we are. No matter the length of time that you've been repeating these ideas to yourself, in reality, it is always changing.

I do not have any doubt in my mind that anyone can change anything they want about their life, whether it is a mental image, physical appearance, or a bad habit. If you're ready to develop the new you read through the fifteen steps below;

-       Have an understanding that there is nothing that can't be changed about your life, even though it looks permanent. Think of the changes that occurred in your life from a younger age until now.

-       Learn that a belief is not the truth but a thought you keep thinking.

-       Have an understanding that our beliefs are not the

truth; they are just things we chose to accept. For example, my favorite color is blue, I'm shy, etc.

-   Have a realization that unless you have the desire to change, the change will never happen.

-   Decide to change. If your decision to change is not deep rooted, real change will elude you.

-   Take gradual steps towards the change you desire. You can run towards the peak of a hill in a flash. You have to take little steps that matter every day. Once you form a habit of taking those steps in the first few weeks, the pattern sticks, and it becomes easy from there on. If what you want to change from is an addiction, gradually reduce the craving. For example, if you're going to quit smoking, gradually reduce the number of cigarettes you smoke every day.

-   Experiment with things that you find easy to change at first; this is to create the belief in yourself that if you can stop doing this, you can stop doing that.

-   Choose something that you always had in mind to change, so that you will appreciate the effectiveness of your new mindset.

-   To make the change real, tell some people close to

you, and give yourself some accountability.

- Ignore the inner critic that keeps telling you that "you can't do this."

- When you mess up, don't give up. It's normal to mess up at times.

- When you slip back into old patterns, make a considerable effort to get out of it. Don't scold yourself; notice it, laugh at it, and try again.

- Don't let the opinions and suggestions of others weigh you down; it will take some time for them to notice the change.

- See yourself as the new you. Feel free to tell others that things are no longer the same. Say to them, "I now exercise everday", "I will not smoke again" etc.

- See the old part of you as a part of you that is gone. If your mind or a friend suggests that you should go back to your old self, say, "That was the old me." If the thoughts keep coming back, distract yourself from them. If a friend keeps suggesting that you revert to your old lifestyle, cut every means of communication with them.

How To Stop Procrastinating And Change Habits

It is true that overthinking leads to procrastination, right? Well, it's also true that procrastination leads to overthinking. Procrastination will have a negative impact on your productivity. Pushing things to a sooner time only increases your anxiety. You will fill your mind with constant worry since you are never sure whether you will complete a particular task or not. Bearing this in mind, it is not surprising that you will find yourself overthinking because you have developed a habit of procrastinating.

About one-fifth of adults procrastinate. Simply put, procrastination refers to the notion of postponing making decisions. Instead of doing something right away, you decide to do it soon. Unfortunately, this takes a toll on you as it leads to reduced productivity, poor mental health, increased worry and stress, etc.

Why Do People Procrastinate?

Have you ever stopped to question yourself why you keep procrastinating even though you know very well that it has a negative impact on how your wellbeing? Indeed, procrastination can increase anxiety simply because you will always struggle to get things done. What's more, you will worry too much about the possibility of failing to accomplish your goals due to wasted time. But why do people procrastinate regardless of the fact that they know what needs to be done?

Undeniably, before dealing with a problem, you have to identify its root cause. Therefore, it is vital that you comprehend the main reasons that push people to procrastinate.

Fear of Failure

One of the main reasons why people procrastinate is because they fear to fail. When one has a gut feeling that they will not do something successfully, it increases the likelihood of postponing their actions. You ought to understand that there is an inherent guarantee that you will not fail because you failed to take action. When you fail to take action, procrastination comes in to comfort you. It protects you from the possibility of failing.

To overcome your fear of failure, you should bear in mind that failing is not the end of everything. It is not fatal. Mistakes are there to help you find another route towards success. This means that failing is part of success. It is crucial that you train yourself to develop a mindset where you believe that not taking any action is the worst thing that you can do. It's better to try and fail than simply do nothing.

Excessive Perfectionism

Perfectionism will also push you to procrastinate. Individuals who consider themselves perfectionists will want to postpone things simply because they believe they will not do certain things perfectly. The effect of having this attitude is that it creates worry since one will not be sure whether they can meet the high-quality standards that they have set for themselves.

The problem with being a perfectionist is that you end up creating unrealistic expectations for yourself. Accordingly, at the end of the day, you will feel that it's better to do nothing because you're not sure of your abilities.

Low Energy Levels

Of course, if you don't have the energy to do something now, there is a good chance that you will want to do it soon. Normally, this is an excuse that is used by individuals with unhealthy lifestyles. They lack vital energy that is required to attend to their day to day routines.

As a solution to this problem, people should strive to be healthy by engaging in physical activity. A healthier lifestyle will boost your productivity since you will enhance your physical and mental health. Ultimately, you will find it easy to make decisions without procrastinating.

Lack of Focus

Your lack of focus will often push you to procrastinate. This is because you don't have a direction to follow when working towards achieving your goals. Failure to have a purpose in life will only make you feel less motivated. The lack of focus affects how you dispel your energy since you will want to do just anything that keeps your mind engaged. At the end of the day, you will find that you have wasted time doing something that adds little or no value to your life. The worst thing is that you end up going to bed feeling guilty about your poor time management. The following morning, the process repeats itself and the cycle continues. Before you know it, you are depressed and lost in your own world.

To overcome this challenge, it is important to set

achievable short term and long-term goals. These can be hourly, daily, weekly or monthly goals. By achieving these goals, you will motivate yourself to work harder towards achieving other larger goals. When setting goals, remember to raise the bar as this ensures that you have something to work hard for. Don't just set goals for the sake of it. Set goals to achieve them.

Disconnect from your Future Self

Another reason why you might be tempted to procrastinate is because there is a disconnect between your present and your future self. A good example of this is being advised to eat healthier. Most people will not heed in to their doctor's recommendations because what they eat now will not directly affect them from the word go. The foods you eat today will affect you more so in the long run. Accordingly, such a disconnect from the future influences people to procrastinate and choose to do something sooner instead of now. The point here is that people will worry less about their present self. Moreover, they will want the future self to worry about what will happen in the future. So, your present self will rarely worry about the consequences of failing to complete a certain task today.

Distractions

Modern-day distractions can also deter you from working productively. In today's world, you will be distracted by emails, social media, text messages, people, etc. Instead of working on a task that you were commissioned to do, you find yourself wasting a lot of time on Facebook, Twitter, Instagram, etc. Before you know it, you have wasted an hour or two on these social media pages. Distractions from the digital world will definitely affect your productivity. In extreme cases, it will lead to stress. This is because you will still have several pending tasks on your to-do list when you finish the workday. Sometimes this might mean that you will need to work overtime to compensate for the time lost. Constantly working overtime is a sign of poor time management.

Avoid this from happening by using your time wisely. Eliminate these distractions by choosing to disconnect yourself from the digital world for some time. After all, there is nothing that you will lose by muting your phone for a couple of hours before checking it.

Negative Effects of Procrastination on Your Life

No one is a stranger to procrastination. At one point in your life, you must have postponed doing something now with the idea of doing it soon. Some people might be less susceptible to procrastination as they can quickly identify that they are procrastinating too much and make the necessary changes. However, others fail to recognize that they are developing a bad habit that could prevent them from reaching their goals. Procrastination can destroy your life in many ways. It's not just about killing time or failing to do certain things immediately. Your life can take a drastic turn that you never anticipated. The following are some effects of procrastination that you ought to be aware of.

Losing Precious Time

When pushing things to attend to them soon, we end up wasting a lot of time. How many hours do you think you have wasted by procrastinating? Say you postpone doing a certain task during your normal workdays. By the end of the week, there is little that you will have achieved. The worst thing about this is that you will have lost precious time. What's more, the time lost cannot be recovered. You'll only live regretting and wishing that you did things on time.

A major problem arises when procrastination becomes a habit. The bitter truth is that you will only realize weeks, months, or years after that time has gone and there is nothing you have done to change your life for the better. Undeniably, any amount of time lost is a lot of time wasted.

You Will Fail to Achieve Your Goals

We work with a rebellious mind. The moment your mind notices that you want to change something in your life, it goes against it. It is for this reason that we often find it difficult to maintain routines. The mind has a mind of its own and it yearns to control itself. So, when you ponder about the fact that you should set goals in your life, your mind will reject such change. As a result, you will find it easy to procrastinate working on the things that you have listed as your goals.

Have you ever wondered by so many people know what to do when it comes to losing weight, but few of them actually do what needs to be done? It's all because of the rebellious mind and our inclination to procrastinate. The more you procrastinate, the more you push your goals away from you. Your life will never be fulfilling if there is nothing worth achieving.

Negative Impact on Your Career

Your career will heavily depend on your performance. By

working towards meeting your goals and your business' goals, there is a good chance that you will succeed in what you do. The company where you work has its own goals. Your productivity is required to make sure that the company meets them. If you are a procrastinator, it becomes difficult to attain these goals. What this means is that you will be sacrificing your career simply because you cannot make desirable actions to act immediately.

Think about it this way, there is a lot that you will miss out on, including promotions and salary raises. When things get out of hand, there is a higher chance that you will lose your job. Therefore, failure to do something about procrastination will be detrimental to your life and your career.

Lower Self-Esteem

One of the reasons why you will push things to a future time is because of low self-esteem. Maybe you are not sure about how to handle a certain assignment. Therefore, you might want to procrastinate so that you can handle it only when you feel ready. What you fail to realize is that procrastination only worsens things as it lowers your self-esteem further. The mere fact that you can't get things done in time will destroy the little self-esteem that you may have in you. Expect your mind to overflow with thoughts of self-doubt. Eventually, this leads to stress and anxiety.

Poor Decision Making

Once you procrastinate, there is a high chance that you will make poor decisions because you will be in a race against time. You will not be thinking clearly. Some of your decisions will require you to think and act fast because of your lack of time. If you hadn't procrastinated in the first place, you wouldn't have the need to make these decisions at such a rapid rate. As such, the quality of the decisions that you will make will be affected greatly. It is also worth mentioning the fact that emotions might cloud your judgment when making impulse decisions. Again, this increases the likelihood of making big mistakes that will cost you in life.

Negative Image

Procrastinating will tarnish your image. Every day, you will find yourself making empty promises that you cannot fulfill. Whether at work or at home, people will begin to perceive you differently. At work, your manager's trust in you will start to deteriorate. Back at home, expect our family to give up on waiting for your empty promises.

Indeed, such effects can have a toll on the quality of your life. This is because your relationships will deteriorate and this will hurt your happiness. Expect this to cause stress and anxiety.

Practical Tips to Beat Procrastination

Now that you understand the causes and effects of procrastination, let's look at how you can beat procrastination with these practical tips.

Divide and Conquer

Instead of allowing a project to overwhelm you because of its demanding nature, you should divide it into smaller chunks that you can easily handle. The same case applies to your goals. Don't set unrealistic goals that will only leave your mind aching. Create smaller attainable goals that you will find it easy to accomplish. Accomplishing these goals will keep you motivated and focused on your dreams.

Forgive Yourself

It's never too late to start again. Successful people can attest to the fact that success is a sum of many mistakes put together. In line with this, if you have been procrastinating for a while now, you should start by forgiving yourself. Empty your mind from the need to worry about your future since there is little that you have been doing about it. Instead, focus your energy on starting fresh. Forgiving yourself helps you to develop a positive attitude towards life once more.

Commit Yourself to the Task

Since you are trying to avoid procrastination, it is imperative that you commit yourself to act instead of avoid. Create a small to-do list that will guide you to do the things that you should do. Work to ensure that you prioritize how you will be handling these tasks without stopping to procrastinate. Remember, it takes practice for you to avoid the urge to postpone things. Hence, a to-do list should remind you of what needs to be done.

Focus on the Reward of Taking Action

It is also important that you understand the potential benefits of doing something now rather than sooner. Therefore, each time you complete a certain task, you should focus on savoring the moment and enjoy how it feels to accomplish something. Doing this more often will help you realize that it is beneficial to take immediate action instead of pushing tasks to a future time or date.

Set Deadlines for Yourself

Additionally, setting deadlines for yourself can make a huge difference towards how you attend to your everyday tasks. It's not a must that you wait for your boss to set deadlines for you. Practice beating procrastination by setting hard deadlines for yourself. If possible, ask a friend to monitor your progress. When setting these deadlines, ensure that you commit yourself to complete them as this is the only way you will avoid the urge to postpone these tasks.

Understand the Reasons for Your Procrastination

Why are you procrastinating in the first place? Well, certainly, this ought to be your starting point when dealing with a habit of procrastination. This requires that you evaluate how you manage your time and your daily tasks. Notice whether there are any particular incidences that push you to procrastinate. Don't just notice them and let them slide. The best way of knowing what affects you is by keeping a record. Write these incidences down in your journal. Maybe it is your constant desire to do things perfectly. Alternatively, it could be that a certain task has overwhelmed you. Writing down these reasons can help you work on them effectively.

Avoid Distractions

Today, digital distractions will be a major reason for your procrastination. Most people don't know how to use their smartphones productively. The worst thing is that it has become a norm that people use their smartphones at work. This makes it difficult to complete pending tasks on time. Therefore, the best thing that you can do is to avoid these distractions. Switch off your phone or mute it to prevent notifications from distracting you. Avoid the urge to check your social media pages while at work.

Reward Yourself

You shouldn't forget to reward yourself for every task that you will accomplish. Find something that you love to do after completing your tasks and reward yourself after successfully accomplishing your mission. The choice of your reward will depend on you. It doesn't have to be something big. Even something small can change how you strive to reach your goals.

Set Your Non-Negotiables

Let's be honest, there are times when you just feel that you don't want to do anything. In such instances, it is important to set your non-negotiables. These are activities that you should do regardless of what happens. Setting these non-negotiables guarantees that you maintain your focus even when you don't feel like it. This helps a lot in maintaining discipline on what should be done.

Procrastination is indeed a thief of time. It not only affects our productivity, but it also has a negative impact on our lives. Usually, it leads to stress, anxiety and in extreme cases, depression. Luckily, this is not a terminal disease. There are plenty of ways in which you can beat procrastination. When using these tips to overcome procrastination, always bear in mind that overcoming procrastination calls for patience and constant practice. So, don't set goals today and forget to do the same the following morning.

How To Stop Worrying And Increase Self-Esteem

There is a strong connection between confidence, emotional control, and the conquering of psychological habits. Over the years, through all of the surveys, interviews, and studies conducted, this is the most common and repeated truth from those participating in them and those performing them: no matter what a person is trying to attempt, confidence is key!

There are lots of different life factors that can affect a person's self-esteem and confidence, with adolescence taking the largest toll on a person's view of themselves. During adolescence, humans It is in these years that men and women receive the majority of their emotional education as it has the highest inclusion of factors like the following for most people:

First romantic relationships (often tumultuous with lots of highs and lows)

• First deep friendships that are tested by adjusting hormones, changing personalities and other life factors that may arise without warning

- First major successes and accomplishments like national awards and recognition, college scholarships and summer internships

- Learning to drive and understanding the responsibility that comes with getting behind the wheel of a car

- Developing decision-making skills that are shaped by how adolescents handle things like peer pressure, balancing their school, work, and social lives, and making their first life-affecting decisions like if they want to further their education after their required schooling is completed

With all of these exciting changes taking place, how could someone's self-esteem and confidence levels be hindered or even damaged? Unfortunately, for all of the positive events men and women experience during their teenage years, there are also a lot of negative events and factors they face (in their highest quantity and intensity than most people see throughout the rest of their lives) such as:

Learning to differentiate affectionate teasing from friends and loved ones with harmful teasing and bullying that comes from those to cause harm

- Physical changes to their skin, muscles and other parts of the body that may require attention from over-the-counter medical products or even prescriptions from medical professionals

- Emotional changes that are often unexpected and out of control as skills are developed through experience and education

- Lots of fear and uncertainty as everything seems to be changing around them without a sense of direction or stopping point insight

Not everyone has come out of adolescence with more negative memories than positive ones, but for those that did and find those negative experiences or memories affecting their adult lives, never fear! There is always action that can be taken to improve your self-esteem and confidence levels to improve your overall life satisfaction and path to reaching your goals!

Self-Esteem & Confidence Levels: How Are They Connected & How Are They Different?

Many times, when people talk about self-esteem and confidence, they speak about them as if they are one and the same. However, in truth, self-esteem and confidence are two separate personality traits that are often interconnected but can be damaged or weakened on their own and need individualized attention to help rebuild and strengthen them.

Pro Tip: Self-awareness is one of the skills people should try to master or at least become more familiar and practiced before turning their energies to self-esteem and confidence. Without knowing where you stand psychologically, mentally, and emotionally, it is difficult to determine where your focus should be aimed and what kinds of goals you should set to reach your ultimate hopes and aspirations.

A Self-Awareness Exercise: Listen to Your Self Talk & Learn from What You Say

One of the best ways for someone to understand their emotional status and why they are feeling a certain way about something is to listen to how they are speaking to themselves, either vocally or in their minds. Everyone has a little voice in their thoughts that voices their opinions about what they are thinking or what they are doing honestly, even if sometimes it can be discouraging or even cruel. The reason this voice can be trusted as a person's most honest thoughts is because these are the thoughts, ideas, and opinions that only circle through someone's mind when they are alone (especially if they are voiced audibly) or whenever they have the opportunity (for those who play the voice in their minds where only they ever hear them).

Those with lower self-esteem and confidence levels often find that their private voice is a negative one, repeating Self Talk that further damages their view of themselves or opinion of their abilities. For this exercise, the goal is to teach individuals how to be more aware of this Self Talk and its tone so that they know how to change their current thought process or emotional status any time their Self Talk takes a negative turn.

When you feel yourself inner voice becoming negative, whether this is because you are unsatisfied with something about your physical appearance or because of a broken sentence in an earlier social interaction, it will start to make critical comments or try to target other fragile or underdeveloped aspects of your personality to bring your mood further down.

• Self-depreciation and attacks on one's own status or abilities are some of the most damaging behaviors someone can take part in, and in many cases, this voice develops subconsciously, only voicing fears and concerns when the brain knows the person is emotionally vulnerable.

• When this behavior starts to take over your thoughts, take a step back and calm your mind. Listen to those thoughts and how your inner voice sounds (or your vocal tone) when the Self Talk starts.

• What kind of tone does your voice or inner voice take?

• Is it angry, sad, or hurtful?

• Does it express any kind of emotion, or does it come across as a more neutral side to your character?

• What kind of words is that voice using?

• Are they offensive?

• Are the words you do not normally use when talking to other people?

• When is this voice most active?

• Does the Self Talk get most negative or most targeted during times of stress? Or any time you are not thinking about something else?

• Do your own thoughts, actions, and behaviors determine how active the voice is? Or is it more active after encounters with others?

Why This Exercise Works?:

This exercise works because it is based around a natural human behavior that all men and women have in common, an inner voice that takes charge of conveying our deepest and most private thoughts about the things we do and say each day. When regularly practiced, it has proven to be one of the most effective exercises in helping people expand their emotional intelligence and their understanding of themselves and how they view their private thoughts.

Whom This Exercise Works Best For?:

This exercise has proven the most effective for those who are dedicated and motivated to take control of their emotional and psychological health. Anyone ready to better understand who they are and what makes them tick to improve their interactions with others or saying yes to more opportunities will also see noticeable progress when this exercise becomes a habit and makes its way into their daily routine.

Once a person becomes comfortable with self-awareness habits and has a better understanding of where their emotional health is, they are better able to make an actionable plan for how to first improve their self-esteem and confidence levels before moving on to more stubborn and difficult to break psychological habits like compulsive overthinking and procrastination. But what is self-esteem, and why is it such an important element to master when it comes to expanding emotional knowledge and health?

What Is Self-Esteem?

Self-esteem is most commonly defined as how a person feels about themselves as a whole. There is often an emotional connection to a person's self-esteem that is not shared with someone's confidence levels.

This trait is one that covers how an individual may feel about:

    Their current life status

- Their current job status

- Their relationship status

- Their main hopes and how they are working toward them

- The people around them like friends and family

- Their physical strengths and where they want to work more

These are just some of the individual factors and variables that can go into shaping a person's view of themselves and their self-esteem. If everyone in the world made a list of the points and traits they think about when they think about their view of themselves, you would most likely see a lot of repeated important factors. However, another certainty that many experts and professionals who study the effects of self-esteem on people are that there will also be as many differences as there are similarities. The reason for this is that everyone has different values or expectations for themselves based on an additional variety of factors such as:

The environment they were raised in

- The family values instilled in them throughout childhood

- Their personal beliefs and values that have developed throughout their individual life experiences

- The expectations they set and the standards they hold themselves and those around them

These are just some of those additional factors that can help to shape an individual. The more in-depth someone looks into their own thoughts, feelings, ideas, hopes, and dreams, the more they will know about themselves, and the higher their self-esteem will grow to be.

Where It Comes From: A person's self-esteem is most commonly shaped by their emotional experiences and encounters. The mistakes, triumphs, accidents, and successes that come throughout life all carry their own emotional and psychological influences with them. It's these influences that are most powerful when it comes to shaping how a person views themselves and their current lifestyle or life situation. The more positive influences and experiences a person can collect, the better their self-esteem will be, and the more emotionally in control they will find themselves when stressful situations arise.

What Is Confidence (or Self-Confidence)?

Confidence (particularly when described as self-confidence) refers to faith a person has in their own knowledge, experience, skills, and abilities. Depending on how much belief someone has in the things they know, the things they say, and the things they do during their personal or professional interactions, the higher a person's confidence levels will be.

Where It Comes From?:

A person's confidence comes from their opinion of and trust in their own strengths and abilities. This trust and faith most often are the result of positive experiences such as promotions at work or awards at school. The more experience they have and proof they have been able to collect that they know what they are doing or what they are talking about, then the higher their self-confidence will be, and the more that will start to affect other areas of their life positively.

There are lots of people who have a high level of self-esteem but find that they lack confidence, especially in certain situations like when they are asked to do something without time to prepare or when they want to ask a question, but are concerned with how others will react to it, so they decide just to keep their hand down. Alternately, people may have high levels of self-confidence and belief in their personal abilities, but also have poor levels of self-esteem from having their heart broken in a failed relationship or from trust issues that developed after being double-crossed by a friend or a co-worker.

Why Are These Traits So Important for Men & Women to Embrace, Develop & Strengthen?

As different as they can be, there are also plenty of situations and experiences that can be caused by interconnected levels of self-esteem and confidence. The more understanding, experienced, and control a person has over their personal self-esteem and confidence levels, the better off they will be in all opportunities they attempt or goals they strive for throughout their life.

Strengthening these traits not only helps with improving a person's overall mental, psychological, and emotional health, but it also comes with a variety of other benefits that can help improve someone's personal health and wellness in a wide range of styles.

The Many Benefits of Building Self-Esteem & Confidence

Even for those who are happy with their control over their habitual overthinking and procrastination, there are an endless number of reasons to keep focused on and motivated to work on for anyone and everyone building self-esteem and confidence levels. Here is a look at some of the most popular and widely reported benefits people have experienced in their quests for higher self-esteem and confidence!

Those with higher self-esteem and personal confidence are less likely to be people pleasers or develop people-pleasing habits than those with lower opinions of themselves or their abilities

- They also tend to have better performance ratings and higher success rates in leadership roles

- Not only are they more personable with customers or other audiences, but they are also more empathetic with employers or co-workers and better able to boost morale during times of high demand or increased stress levels

- They are also more likely to have higher success rates with setting and reaching personal and professional goals because they are more self-aware of their mental, psychological, emotional changes and how it affects their daily performance

- Those with higher self-esteem and confidence levels report more personal and professional satisfaction throughout their lives

- They are more likely to take up opportunities when offered

- They also tend to be bolder and more dominant in their professional teams and social circles as they are more likely to openly share their opinions and start conversations with even those they do not know with more confidence than those who question themselves and hesitate around others

These are just a handful of the benefits that study and research subjects of all ages and lifestyles have reported when tracked over time and throughout their personal improvement journey! Each person will find a whole new array of benefits and progress markers that are specialized and more tailored to their individual needs based on the techniques they choose to put into practice, how dedicated they can remain to their self-improvement plan and of course, what specific issues and concerns that are working to improve or eliminate.

How to Get Started with Building Self-Esteem & Confidence Levels

Like with developing any new positive habits to replace the damaging negative ones, the first step to getting started revolves around a person's self-awareness of their thoughts and emotions. The first thing anyone should do when trying to build their self-confidence and self-esteem is to take a look at their points of strength and points of concern. The following is an example of a self-awareness exercise that many people have reported progress during their own quests for higher self-esteem.

A Self-Awareness Exercise: Get to Know Yourself & Your Restrictions

This self-awareness exercise is one of the most basic, one of the most widely used and one of the most effective, proven techniques for anyone trying to get a better idea of their personal highs and points where they may want to work on improving to make the most of their personal potential.

Set aside a time where you can clear your mind and focus on the concerns at hand

• Make sure to deal with any potential distractions such as silencing your cell phone and turning off your television, perhaps even closing the door to the room you are going to be contemplating in so that you are not interrupted by anyone else in the building

• Layout a clean piece of paper and get the kind of pens that you when working on organizational thinking

• For some, they may just use a basic blue or black pen for anything they need to write, but when it comes to organization, some people prefer multiple colors or types of tips to choose from to separate different thoughts, ideas or options into color-coded or differently shaped areas

• Make a list of your strengths

• This can be emotional strengths like being able to remain calm in high-stress situations or always responding to friends and family the same day they message you

• This can be professional strengths like mastering a certain skill or getting recognition for something you accomplished in your department

• This can be personal strengths like organization and discipline, anything that you take pride in and use regularly

• Now flip the paper over or draw a line to separate your lists and make a list of your weaker points or skills that you want to develop and master

• Again, these points can be emotional like a tendency to breakdown when challenges arise in your personal or professional life

• They can be professional points of concern like wanting to be better at communicating with customers or being bolder when it comes to discussing a promotion with your employer

• They can also be personal, like a bad habit snapping at people who speak to you early in the morning or late in the day

• You do not have to make lists!

• Some people find that this exercise works better when they form connecting circles of related thoughts or pie charts of strengths, weaknesses and action plans

• The point is not to force your mind to start thinking in lists, but rather to find a way to organize your thoughts related to personal strengths, weaknesses, and goals for self-improvement.

How To Be More Positive (Step By Step Process)

Meditation is an amazing way of calming the mind and building the focus in the right direction. Meditation can help in calming even the most agitated minds. It brings clarity of thoughts and helps you look at things from a broader perspective.

Meditation is thousands of years old practice and has been followed religiously in eastern cultures. It is very useful for relaxing the mind, sharpening focus, and increasing awareness. All these three things ultimately help you in lowering anxiety and putting a stop to overthinking things.

Many people think that meditation may increase overthinking as you allow the mind to ponder over things for even longer. However, that's not true as when you meditate, you become more mindful and you are able to look at the problems with considerable detachments.

Detachment makes all the difference in the way we perceive problems. When we feel too identified with the problem, we are not looking deep inside but trying to find an escape route. When you are looking with detachment, you are able to observe the root cause of the problem and that takes you near the solution.

Most of the time, the problems that we feel are very big in our lives have no significance at all. If there was a person who was very cruel or abusive to you in your childhood, there is a great likelihood that he would invoke the same feelings even when you grow up. This can happen despite the fact that you may have grown bigger, more powerful, and wield more authority now.

Do you know how they tie elephants in India?

They dig a small peg in the ground and tie the elephant to it with a thin rope. That rope can't keep the elephant tied. Yet, the elephants never try to break that rope. Do you know the reason why?

When the elephants are very young, they are tied with similar ropes. At that time, the ropes are powerful enough to hold them. However, despite the fact that the elephants grow at a phenomenal rate, their mind is never able to grow out of the power of that rope. This is how fears generally work.

Meditation can help you in analyzing the mind and finding irrational fears that might be causing stress and anxiety.

How Can Meditation Help?

Meditation can give you the right process to look at the problems. It will provide you the firm rooting where you won't feel scared of the issues causing anxiety.

It also helps you in addressing the events in the past that trigger anxiety and fear. You are able to unload the baggage of the past and understand the ways in which your thought process works.

It is a very simple practice that doesn't require rigorous training or outside help. You only need to be in constant touch of your own self. The technique is important, but that is only a smaller part of meditation, the bigger part of meditation is your ability to get in touch with your own self. Once you are able to establish a strong connection, the things that cause anxiety don't remain significant.

Meditation is an excellent practice for people who are suffering from stress, anxiety, depression, internal chaos, and fears.

What Kinds of Meditations Can Help?

There are dozens of types of meditation techniques that are focused on various goals. Some help you in becoming more mindful while others help you in relaxing the mind completely. There are meditations for making you feel more grateful towards the world, while others can help you in creating resting awareness where your mind can truly rest.

Some important meditation techniques that can help in easing stress and anxiety are:

Body Scan Meditation

This meditation technique is also called a progressive relaxation technique. It helps you in addressing the problems in your body. Stress and anxiety can lead to stiffness and pain in the body. You might find it difficult to complete the usual tasks in the day without feeling the pain. This stress can make you ache for relief. Body scan meditation is a very soothing practice in which you address the areas of pain in your body through your awareness. You acknowledge and accept whatever is causing the pain, and your awareness helps in easing the pain. This meditation technique is very helpful in relieving pain. It also helps in calming the mind and you are able to get a better understanding of your fears.

Focused Attention

This meditation technique uses the breath as the anchor to bring your awareness to a single point. You are able to anchor your mind better, and getting hold of your racing thoughts becomes easy. You can do this meditation anywhere and it is very helpful in case you are feeling frightened or anxious.

You are able to become consciously aware of your thoughts and stop your mind from wandering here and there.

Acknowledgement

This meditation technique is especially very helpful if you are trying to run away from your fears, and they are getting stronger by the day. It gives you an opportunity to acknowledge all the feelings in your mind and accept them. You are able to register everything that's going on inside you and hence the darkness of ignorance fades away.

It is very helpful in clearing the mishmash of emotions, and you are able to note the things that are disturbing you in reality. You must remember that acknowledgment of the problem is the first step towards solving it effectively.

Acknowledgment of the thought also helps you in clearing the clutter in the mind and makes it possible for you to let go of the things that are solving no purpose in your memory.

Visualization

With the help of certain imageries, you can distract your mind from the existing negative chain of thoughts and plant a positive message in your mind. Our mind works very efficiently on subtle hints, and hence whatever you feel is easily incorporated in the mind.

Loving-Kindness Meditation

This meditation technique is very helpful in case you are stressed and anxious about certain people. People from our past and present have a deep impact on our life. Some people can have a very deep and disturbing impact on our life. Their actions can leave very deep wounds that may not heal even after years. We form grudges against such people and then get stuck in the cycle of carrying that grudge forever. Simply the burden of the memories keeps the wounds alive forever. We also find it really difficult to trust others or lead a normal life.

This meditation technique can help in getting over such trauma. It gives us a chance to move on in life and make new and better memories. This is one of the best meditation techniques to bring peace in life and heal the wounds.

Reflection

This meditation technique helps in finding answers hidden deep inside our minds. There are several things that we simply assume without applying any logic to them. There are certain fears that have no place to be, but they thrive in our minds as we seldom pay attention to them.

This technique helps you in reflecting on the problems and addressing them in a logical way. You get a chance to reflect upon the perceived problems and lower the burden of stress and anxiety on your mind.

Resting Awareness

In this meditation technique, you don't fight your thoughts, you allow the thoughts to enter but don't get affected by them. You maintain a resting awareness of the thoughts and observe their genesis and end. This can help you in getting out of the clutches of your disturbing thoughts that overpower you anytime.

How to Practice Meditation?

People have strange notions about meditation. They feel that to mediate; you need to sit in specific contorted postures for hours and chant mantras that you don't understand. Meditation is a way of life. It can be practiced in any form and posture you like. There are some simple rules that you must follow as they help you in building focus and prevent you from falling in the trap of negative emotions.

When and Where to Practice

There are certain meditation practices that help in lowering stress, and they can be practiced anytime you feel stress and anxiety taking over your mind.

Certain meditation practices like the body scan meditation work best when you can get in specific positions. Like the body scan meditation should be carried out at the end of the day lying flat on your bed or a mat. Loving-kindness meditation should be practiced early in the morning for making you feel better throughout the day. Keeping such things in mind can help you in getting the most out of your meditation practice. This doesn't mean that these meditation techniques can't be practiced at other times of the day. It only means that during these times, they are more effective.

Duration

There can be no diktat about the duration of meditation practice. In the beginning, you may face problems even in sitting straight for 5-10 minutes in a stretch. The mind would be very volatile, and it would keep tripping you down. However, as you practice, you get used to the routine, and you are able to meditate for much longer without losing your focus.

The duration should be as per your convenience. However, in the initial days, you should try to progressively increase the duration of your meditation sessions. It is said that if you practice meditation continuously for 48 hours around the same time, your body gets used to the routine, and you would face no difficulty in making it a part of your life.

Posture

Some people have great apprehensions about the sitting posture. They feel that they can't sit in cross-legged postures for too long. Some people that they can't sit in cross-legged posture at all due to health issues or their weight.

You can practice meditation sitting in a cross-legged posture, sitting on a chair, lying down, standing, walking, and running. It is your focus of the mind that matters the most and not the way you fold your legs.

Sitting in a specific posture like the cross-legged posture

definitely has a positive effect. There are certain pressure points that get pressed, and they help in maintaining greater focus and awareness. However, your inability to sit in those postures should prevent you from getting benefits of meditation at all.

Pro-Tips

Always Keep Your Spine Straight

This is one of the most important rules that you must follow while meditating. Either you are practicing meditation in sitting, standing, or lying position, your spine should always be straight. You shouldn't be bending sideways or slouching to your back or leaning forward. Not keeping the spine straight will affect your focus and may make you feel distracted, sleepy, or even fearful.

For instance, leaning forward while meditating can lead to the formation of depressing thoughts. Your anxiety levels would shoot up, and you'd find it very hard to remain focused on any particular thing.

Bending backward will make you feel restless.

If you tilt to your right, you might start feeling sleepy. Tilting to your left may lead to an increase in your sexual desires, and hence focus on the mind would get difficult.

You Can Use a Backrest

If you are practicing meditation in a seated position, you can use backrest to keep your spine straight. Supporting your spine is not a problem in meditation. You only need to ensure that your spine remains upright, and you don't bed your back.

Don't Use a Neckrest

Using a neck rest is very bad in meditation, as in that case, you will lose control of your thoughts. You have to keep your neck straight and you can't use a pillow. Your neck needs to remain unsupported if you want to have active control of your thoughts. Using neck rest also creates the danger of drifting into sleep.

Rest Your Hands Comfortably

You can rest your hands in a comfortable position. There is no need to keep them on your knees or in any other specific position.

Don't Overstress Your Body and the Mind

Meditation is a relaxing activity, and it shouldn't become a punishment for the body or the mind. You must practice meditation only for as long as you feel comfortable.

Practicing 5 minutes more than you usually practice is not a problem but forcing yourself to practice for hours can prove to be counterproductive.

Even if you want to increase your meditation time, break it into smaller parts if your body or the mind is not feeling comfortable. In place of having an hour-long session, you can have two sessions of half-an-hour each. Your aim should be to achieve greater balance, focus, and awareness.

Meditation is an age-old, time-tested way to bring clarity in mind and increase awareness. It can help in lowering anxiety and stress levels. If you feel troubled by your thoughts and your mind has fears that come to haunt you anytime, meditation can provide you the answers to most of your problems and you must definitely give it a try.

Mindfulness

Mindfulness is a great way to get out of the vicious cycle of negative thinking. Mindfulness helps you to stay grounded in reality. You are able to understand your limitations clearly and get a chance to work slowly toward improving them. Mindfulness is a process of continuous improvement. It also helps you in getting free from the baggage of past experiences, and hence you are able to try fresh every time.

You can try mindfulness meditation to prevent the formation of negative thoughts in your mind.

Thought-Modification through Cognitive Behavioral Therapy

Cognitive Behavioral Therapy is based on the concept that our feelings, actions, thoughts, and physical sensations are interconnected and changing one can help in changing others.

It can help you in reducing stress and coping with complicated relationships. You may find it easier to deal with grief in life or face other tough challenges in life.

This is a way to modify the way our conscious mind work. This therapy doesn't have any effect on the subconscious mind, but it is able to affect the way our conscious mind thinks and perceives things.

Mindfulness in Everyday Life

There is no law that restricts you to practice mindfulness while sitting on the floor or on a chair. You can practice mindfulness in your everyday life by being mindful about what you are doing. Below is a look at how you can apply mindfulness to your daily routine.

Washing the Dishes

Usually, most people will want to take advantage of the process of washing dishes to chat or watch a TV show. However, this alone time can be used to practice mindfulness. How do you do this? Immerse yourself in the process. Don't take anything for granted that is happening when you're cleaning the dishes. Notice the warm or cold water you are using. Pay attention to the sounds of the pans and other dishes that you are washing. Try your best to be present in the moment. Don't just wash the dishes for the sake of it. Wash them while taking time to experience everything that is happening around you.

Driving

There are many instances where you may find yourself zoning out when driving. Most people spend their time thinking about what they did during the day. When driving home from work, some folks will use this time to think about what they will be eating for dinner. Practicing mindfulness can help you maintain your focus on the immediate environment around you.

First, if the radio is playing, turn it off. Alternatively, you can choose to play some soothing music that will help you meditate. While maintaining your focus on the wheel, practice breathing exercises as you pay attention to your bodily movements. Practicing this regularly can help prevent your mind from wandering.

Brushing Your Teeth

You can also take advantage of your daily routine of brushing your teeth to practice mindfulness. The main thing that you should pay attention to is your body. Notice how your feet are connected to the floor. Do you feel cold since you are barefoot on the cold tiles? Think about the way you're holding the toothbrush in your hand and how your arm is moving sideways or up and down to clean your teeth.

Judging from the everyday mindfulness exercises mentioned, it is clear that living mindfully is all about living in the present moment. Sometimes we find ourselves overthinking because we cannot control our minds when they are left to their own devices. Therefore, it is by being present in every moment that you can catch yourself overthinking and stop it.

How Mindfulness Can Help You Deal with Anxiety

When you learn to live mindfully, you will be more observant about what goes on around you. This means that your mind will be able to think clearly and identify situations or triggers that can make you anxious. The following are ways in which mindfulness can help you manage anxiety.

Where Thoughts are Born And Why

When we worry about something that has not yet happened, we focus all our energy on anticipating something that might never happen. In this way, we occupy our mind with negative thoughts that have no other result than to attract other negativity.

When we are worried, we do not fully live the present and, furthermore, we cloud the experiences we are experiencing due to our pessimistic vision. In fact, most of our concerns have to do with something we have no control over. We can, therefore, worry as much as we want, but this will not solve the problem in any way, indeed: most of the time, what we are so concerned with will not turn out to be as terrible as we imagined.

Excessive worry easily turns into anxiety, fear of what we do not know and of the future. In this way, worries affect both our physical and emotional health, leading to stress and anxiety disorders. When we live constantly worried, our body is in a state of continuous alert, as if it were always in danger; this condition, on the other hand, should only occur sometimes and not often.

Little by little, therefore, we lose the ability to evaluate situations objectively, and we take for granted that life hides many dangers; in this way, we preclude the possibility of relaxing and enjoying beautiful things. We live every situation as a conflict or something to resolve, even when it comes to insignificant commitments.

The concerns are both unnecessary and harmful. This evidence known to most people does not always protect us from the anxiety we feel about something that is about to happen. Near an important date, it sometimes happens to be struck by an irrational fear that leads to making rash choices, to assume a suspicious and hypercritical attitude, to conceive of little objective and defeatist thoughts. What brain mechanisms regulate this complex function? What role does the individual will play in the management of this psychic experience?

According to the research conducted by Dr. Joseph LeDoux at the University of New York, the repercussions of the aforementioned mental ruminations on the well-being experienced would be very strong since the reaction generated by a situation that causes apprehension is hardly composed and balanced. In fact, we tend to exaggerate when we find ourselves thinking about what awaits us self-inflicting us with weary psychological suffering.

However, science provides us with an excuse for not attributing total responsibility for the illness to the person's will. The amygdala treats and evaluates incoming stimuli responding to a possible danger with the release of some neurotransmitters, such as dopamine, capable of producing a generalized alert state. The information is then transmitted to the encephalic cortex, which processes the received information in a logical and rational manner.

Emotions are, therefore, as reiterated by LeDoux, generated before thought. The latter often fails to impose itself on the affective flux already triggered leaving us at the mercy of our troubles.

The suffering that we perceive in such situations is revealed, therefore, real and responsive to precise encephalic mechanisms. Furthermore, if the aforementioned condition persists, we may encounter cognitive, attentive, and decision-making problems. Such widespread impairment of intellectual faculties will not only affect the quality of the behaviors acted out, but also the lucidity and objectivity experienced by the subject.

Knowing how to manage what we feel is not at all easy. Sometimes the approach of an event that is very important to us cannot leave us indifferent. However, it is necessary to recognize the value we attribute to it and the apprehension that it gives us, because of the success of the activity we care so much about. Only by openly facing our experiences can we not remain a victim and bring home the desired result.

I don't know people who have never worried about something in their lives. Whether it's a job interview, a question at school, a plane trip, a health problem, or something more trivial, we all had a moment of anxiety.

This becomes our unique and pounding thought for whole days and prevents us from serenely carrying out our activities, which is why it is fundamental to learn to stop worrying excessively about something before this state of mind turns into a real pathology

Worry is a "thought that occupies our mind" generating anxiety, restlessness, tension, problems in sleep. Let's try together to understand what it is.

The concern is the main component of all anxiety and depression disorders. For this reason, it seems appropriate to observe this phenomenon to prevent and promote our psychological health.

There are different types of concerns; each of us can experience one or more of these in our lives (Leahy 2005):

- being rejected
- being alone
- making an exam wrong
- not looking pleasant
- what other people think of us
- getting sick
- falling from a height
- having a plane crash
- losing your money
- being late
- going crazy
- having thoughts and strange sensations

- to be humiliated

The concerns are, therefore accompanied by thoughts on the concerns themselves. We can often tell ourselves that "we know that we are expecting the worst, but we cannot fail to do it" or "even if people tell me that all is well I cannot stop worrying."

We, therefore, come to believe that we cannot control our thoughts and that this could be a problem for our mental health.

Where It Originates From

According to the researches, having experimented in their environment of growth, life history and learning about traumas linked to the threat of their physical health can contribute to the onset of experiences of concern (of various kinds) in adulthood. The significant family models characterized by concern and hyper-protection often provide conditioning and reinforcement of the use of these strategies (the outside world is dangerous).

In these environments of growth, there seems to be difficulty in the expression of emotions and in providing a warm and safe environment. In some cases, children find themselves parents of their parents. A loss of the parent before the age of 16 and in general, a type of attachment with insecure family members they produce a living environment that is perceived as risky and a source of alarm.

Even shame is a very significant issue in keeping the trend worry. In a situation whereby we hear " what they think of you? " The message we receive is that what we are or do must be hidden and not shared, because it would not be accepted.

Because we worry

The reason we use concern is that this strategy seems to make sense to us.

We can believe that in this way we will find a solution. In some cases, it may seem that worrying allows us not to forget things. Generally, the worry is intended to anticipate and may diminish the feeling of getting unprepared for events.

A rather interesting thing is the socially acceptable meaning that can convey the concern: if I worry it means that I am a responsible person and this will make me appreciable by others.

People don't want to worry. It is certainly not their main purpose. The concern is a means of facing situations that we consider dangerous, uncertain, out of control.

The reason why we worry is that we believe we must do it:

- we believe that concern helps us solve problems

- we believe that the world is dangerous and that we do not have the resources to face it

- we believe that concern helps us to avoid thinking about the worst possible consequences of an event

- we believe that worry keeps us safe from too strong emotions

- we believe that concern contains our anxiety

- we believe we have control

- we believe we are more responsible

- we believe we are reducing uncertainties

- we believe we control thoughts and emotions

- we believe we have more motivation

But does all this work?

Our mind is not used to falsify. This means that we are inclined to use the knowledge we have learned and not to question it so easily. All this has an "economic" meaning. We save energy. But it can be a fallacious strategy. In some cases, it is necessary to collect information to verify or falsify our ideas.

"If I am certain that riding a bicycle is dangerous, I will never try to give it a try. The worry is so strong that I cannot allow myself to experiment."

In this case, we can immediately observe how concern, rather than motivating our intentionality, tends to limit it and lead us to procrastinate important things.

In short, the concern seems to produce problems instead of diminishing them.

Some thoughts on this:

I am sure that all this will seem familiar to those who have experienced the concern. Surely you have done your best to try to counter it. But it didn't always work. Sometimes what seems to help us is instead something that keeps the problem itself.

Change Habits

In order to gather how to change your habits and actions towards positivity, we need to first appreciate what is positive thinking. Positivity entails the mental process that refocuses our emotions towards optimism. These people are often inclined to always think the best out of any situation. They would not focus mostly on the negative side, even if the results are not the way they expected. A positive mindset is a behavior or a state of mind that keeps recurring. Many people trying to achieve a positive mindset are often drawn to the fact that this is not a onetime thing and that its nature is cyclical. Whenever you find yourself in a situation that is demanding. A positive mindset will always seek the best out of every situation. In order to achieve positive thinking, you ought to embrace positivity at its finest. Most of us forget that positivity sits at the helm of a positive mindset.

Positivity goes beyond the personal attributes of having a face that suggests that you are cheerful and happy. It encompasses the overall outlook that we give to life. The way we generally look at life will work a great deal in determining our focus in life. A positive minded individual will have less focus on what tends to annoy them in life. Their energies are redirected to what works for them, what makes them happy. In order to embrace positivity, one needs to understand that challenges are part of life and learning to embrace them and live with them is one step towards achieving your goal. A mindset, from the wording of it, refers to the situation that you decide to put your mind in. In order for one to be referred to as to have embraced positivity, there are a number of pointers that manifest themselves. Some of these pointers are:

Optimistic Mindset

Embracing optimism acts as the first stage towards achieving positivity. Optimism can be said to a synonym of positivity in that they both have the same effect. Optimism is the act of expecting every outcome to impress you, and when this does not happen, you will find happiness in every situation you may be in. The opposite of optimistic is pessimistic. A pessimist is an individual who only visualizes the bad in every situation. They are often inclined to negativity. Time and again, it has been a bone of contention that people with a negated mindset are always prone to accept results the way they are because if it is not a loss, then it is a win, and surely it still works for you. However, this is not the case as when an optimist is faced with a loss. They will find a way to make it work for themselves even in that time of need. Positive minded people have the tendency of giving it a shot rather than dismissing it entirely.

Maturity

Maturity here exhibits itself in a manner that suggests that you are accepting that things may not always happen in a manner that you want them to. Accepting the factors and consequences of the occurrence is what helps a great deal in making your move on. In order to achieve this, we need to appreciate that we are prone to making mistakes, and when this happens, we should build upon our mistakes rather than letting them affect us entirely.

The Heart of Resilience

You will be pulled down emotionally almost every time when your plans do not go through, or maybe the outcome was undesired. People who let this kind of energy burn them from the inside will always have a resulting effect of feeling low. Having maturity as your guide is one way to ensure that you get through this peacefully. In order to get back from an occurrence that was painful to you, one needs to understand the fact that letting this feeling pin you down will not work best for you. You have to come off your comfort zone and make sure that you are getting rid of all the negative energy that needs to be channeled in the way that makes you happy.

Gratefulness

When something happens, that is in your favor, and you ought to find it in your heart to say thank you. Good things have a sense of rarity, which makes them gold. Whenever a good thing happens to you, no matter how frequent, it is good practice and behavior to always say thank you. This should be done in a continuous manner.

Having a Present Mind

Absent-minded people have the tendency to build castles in the air; thus they will stumble upon any thought just to pass the time. These are the type of people who tend to think in a negated manner. When you are present in mind, this means that you will be conscious of any arising factor and that whenever this happens, you will be ready in your mind to face it.

Being Integral

A person who is integral is an individual who embraces integrity. Integrity refers to the act of doing what is right and sticking to it. You are honorable about your failure, no matter how low you fall. Some people have the tendency of lying to themselves about a pre-determined facet in life. This is often not advisable as the reality will always dawn one way or another.

However, there are ways in which an individual may achieve a positive mindset. This is through embracing positivity every step of the way. The transformative steps towards being positive minded include:

- Commence Your Day with a Positive Attitude

The way you commence your day will determine how best you will operate throughout the day. When your day is distorted at its onset, this is a pointer that the rest of the day is going to follow suit. It is not dependent on the fact that you have bad luck but rather dependent on a much bigger perspective. People who have a rough start at the onset of the day tend to link this to the rest of the day. Thus, in turn, the day looks to be a wholesome boring spree yet it is your perception that effects this. In order to make sure that you are devoid of this, you ought to start your day by having a monologue with yourself. In order to achieve this, the mirror is your biggest tool. Take a moment and look into the mirror. Tell yourself that the day will be successful and in turn, channel this energy throughout the rest of the day.

- Radar on Positivity No Matter How Remote

As part of life, obstacles come in to create challenges that make our lives more adventurous. These obstacles will always manifest themselves, whether we like it or not. Getting through an obstacle will be the biggest determinant of how you move on. You are encountered with a problem; for instance, what you need to do is focus on the minute facets that bring about happiness and joy to you. For instance, you can make a joke out of the worst scenario possible. This brings in a light mood.

- Your Mistakes Should Be Your Biggest Lessons

When you make a mistake, you should not be overwhelmed by the consequences of the mistake, no matter how dire they might see. Falling down will necessarily determine how you rise. Focus on your mistakes; let them form part of you. Tell yourself that you are not going to fall for these mistakes ever again. With this in place, device new methods of getting through the day.

- Be Transformative

Transformation here involves two facets, one is the positive thoughts, and the other one is the negated one. This transformation should assume a manner that it should be from the negative to the positive. Never should you adopt the vice versa because it is a downhill road. Avoid putting yourself down in that you are telling yourself you cannot do something because you are not good at it. A rather different approach to this would be challenging yourself in order to be the best in what may seem subtle to you at the moment.

- Take Note of the Present

Negativity draws its base from sentiments that might have been expressed by an individual, for instance, of higher hierarchy than you. It may be that your boss has scolded you for the occurrence of something particular. You ought not to think deeply about these sentiments because the deeper you go, the severe the effects are. Take a point of not holding on to the bad energy. Do this by releasing yourself from the shackles of bad thoughts. You can decide to erase this from your mind as soon as it is done and move on to be mindful of what is in the present.

Believe you can and you're halfway there.

Theodore Roosevelt

CONCLUSION

Elevation, thought as the sense that you get once you find somebody doing an act of kindness, jealousy, or even inner goodness, induce one to desire to similar actions. Altruism, usually known to be an act of selflessness and generosity to the others, but could additionally describe the sensation you will get from helping others. Satisfaction, thought as an awareness of pride and pleasure you make it from attaining some thing or meeting a necessity. Relief, thought as the impression of happiness you go through once an uncertain situation ends up to your very best, or perhaps a poor effect is avoided. Affection, thought as a psychological attachment to somebody (if not a pet), followed closely with a liking for these and also a feeling of joy in their own company. Cheerfulness, thought as an atmosphere of brightness, being optimistic and clearly joyful or chipper; sense like what's moving your own way. Surprise (the fantastic sort of surprise), characterized as an awareness of delight whenever someone brings you unexpected enjoyment or perhaps a situation goes much better than you'd expected. Psychotherapy, characterized as an emotion between a strong awareness of self-esteem and belief on your own; could be specific to some circumstance or activity, or even maybe more universal. Admiration, thought as an atmosphere of hot endorsement, admiration, and admiration for something or somebody. Enthusiasm, thought as an expression of enthusiasm, followed closely by motivation and participation. Eagerness, thought as a less intense type of excitement; an atmosphere of openness and enthusiasm for something. Euphoria, thought as intense and all-encompassing awareness of happiness or joy, frequently experienced if something exceptionally favorable and stimulating happens.

Contentment, thought as calm, reassuring, and low-key awareness of happiness and wellbeing. Enjoyment, thought as an atmosphere of shooting pleasure in what exactly is happening around you, particularly in situations such as a leisure activity or social gathering. Optimism, thought as positive and optimistic emotion which motivates one to enjoy a bright future, one where you think things will probably mostly workout. Happiness, thought as an atmosphere of joy and pride from how things are moving; an overall awareness of joy of and excitement for a lifetime. Love is possibly the most powerful of most positive emotions and love is just a sense of profound and enduring affection for somebody, together with a willingness to place their needs in front of one's; it could be guided towards a person, a set, and sometimes all humankind. Love may be your most powerful positive emotion plus it may possibly be the most powerful cure for over-thinking and stress.

To check or cure over-thinking disease and stress, shortness of unwanted emotions need to become disentangled. Favorable feelings balance together with all intellectual capacity of mind that over-thinking will not happen all of the time. Strong constructive emotions, particularly love, have become crucial for the wellness of the mind, health of manifestation and production of both productive and well-coordinated notions.

The Vicious Cycle Of Worrying

It's Not Beware; It's Be Aware

Contrary reasoning issue is disarranged that branch from extreme nervousness and is most usually named as tension issue. Under this specific sort of turmoil are disarranges like over the top urgent issue, summed up tension issue, post-horrendous pressure, alarm issue, and social fear. It's the contrary reasoning in these negative reasoning issue or nervousness issue that feeds the uneasiness making it develop. This issue is established in our considerations. To fix it, we should change our negative musings into positive ones with ways like subjective treatment.

It's All the Same and Holding On

People who experience the evil impacts of such contrary reasoning issue trust that everything will remain the equivalent and it would dependably be awful - nothing changes. By taking such a conviction into their arrangement of reasoning, they're shutting entryways or approaches to get help. Treatment for such issue is a usual procedure and by clutching their point.

Discussing hanging tight, with these sorts of disarranges, individuals experiencing it clutch damaging or horrendous encounters. Like this, they make it harder for themselves to get away from the endless loop of antagonism and nervousness. These negative musings are the fundamental power wellspring of these scatters as they are never-ending being an idea of. It's one thing to clutch a memory, yet another circumstance totally when you fixate on it and fall caught to a destructive idea cycle. In addition to the fact that it interrupts your everyday life, it additionally alters your rationale and may make you avoid certain circumstances and in actuality constrain you.

Absolutes

Those experiencing contrary reasoning issue think in absolutes or limits. They see that there must be a terrible or decent circumstance. This can be especially hard to manage as they, as a rule, see the negative piece of things more and amplify them, eclipsing whatever positive there is. To change by the typical idea, they should comprehend that stressing is typical to a degree and that there would dependably be upsides and downsides or tremendous and awful in the circumstances. They should realize that whatever con or terrible there is ought not to control or restrict them. They should discover what it is that is causing them the fits of anxiety and fanatical reasoning and abstain from inclination defenseless or powerless. We should all understand that we are in charge.

Contrary reasoning issue may take various structures and extents, yet one component remains the equivalent - the contrary reasoning. The drug may help; however, by the day's end, whatever occurs, it's something we need to deal with in our brains. Early mediation is ideal and is available to treatment would ensure that advancement would move along as it should. Life is great, it may not be simple, but instead, it is excellent. Find it.

Habitual Thinking Disorder

Battle It!

It happens over and over and once more. Your contemplations appear to spin around very similar things over and over. It's expending you gradually. You endeavor to rest. However, you can't. There's a humming, a pestering, an irritating voice in your mind that won't give you harmony. It frequents you. You can't complete anything. You realize it needs to stop. This, old buddy, is the indication of the formal reasoning issue.

I'll Never Get over It.

Getting over the impulsive reasoning issue is an assignment with the trouble that is equal to its seriousness. A couple of troubling musings are satisfactory and particularly typical. Having considerations that appear to assume control over your life; however, giving it a chance to leave you speechless as opposed to moving relentlessly forward is very unfortunate. It's downright awful when you let it drag you to the past and keep you there.

All things being equal, it is anything but difficult to overcome this issue. You truly need to need it, and you should be eager to focus on beating it because there's a straightforward arrangement that can posture to be extremely troublesome if you go on about it with the methods for an enthusiastic reasoning issue. What's going on here? It's merely to concentrate on positive contemplations and have faith in them. Make a decent attempt to bring yourself harmony. Once more, everything's more complicated than one might expect, particularly with a positive frame of mind conceived from this issue.

Goodness Yeah? So, what's the Plan?

The best arrangement you could need to overcome mechanical reasoning issue is to endeavor to slaughter each negative idea when it comes. When you see that your musings are beginning to get sharp, go for a positive reply. You can believe, "I'm not going to have a ton of fun at the gathering" at that point go "however, on the other hand, my companions are there so it'll be alright. It very well may be more than alright." It might be challenging to do at first from its sheer newness, and how it's so inverse to what you're utilized to, yet like-minded all abilities, all you need is a touch of training. Help yourself out and don't lose heart with this one. The more you do it, the more straightforward it gets and the more it'd appear to be a programmed reflex.

Beating critical reasoning issue is your opportunity not merely to better your state of mind or yourself as an individual, yet it can better your life when all is said in done. Before long you'd discover things looking into your way and that you're getting to places you need to be throughout everyday life. Escape the shadows; see life in a different light.

Positive or Negative Thinking

As of now, you can discover sufficient proof to demonstrate that your life is hopeless, exhausting, and discouraging. You can likewise create evidence to prove that your life is happy and energizing.

We should complete an activity!

Check out the room you are in. Do you see any residue and soil? Any turmoil? A storage room or drawers that need arranging? A heap of papers that ought to be recorded or reused? Does the room need paint or fix? Is the light switch plate smeared?

How would you feel? Did you discover enough proof that life is dreadful, discouraging, and an excessive amount to deal with?

Check out the room once more. Do you see something given by a companion or relative that is exceptional to you? Does it bring sweet recollections? If you are perched on an agreeable seat? Do you have a PC to keep in contact with companions and become familiar with a wide range of energizing things? Do you have flooring that is more pleasant than an earth floor? Anything there that produces music for you? Compact disc player, radio? It isn't great that we can flip that switch and have light whenever of day or night?

How would you feel now? Did you discover enough proof that life is fantastic, brilliant, and brimming with beneficial things?

Our musings are powerful! Those musings control hormones in our body, and those hormones make us feel better or awful. They additionally decide if we have great wellbeing or horrendous wellbeing, regardless of whether we are discouraged or euphoric.

Indeed, there is a concoction irregularity when individuals are discouraged, yet we should inquire as to why? God did not make us that way. There is lot of research out there on what considerations to do our wellbeing.

If you checked out the room and didn't discover anything significant that didn't come without a miserable or negative idea, I would state that you don't feel sound in that condition of reasoning. It takes a noteworthy upgrade to get your "stinking reasoning" out the entryway, yet you can do it!

Shouldn't something be said about positive reasoning? That can be similarly as awful for you!

Positive scholars now and again utilize positive reasoning as an approach to legitimize their failure to acknowledge the occasion. They have a considerable rundown of "should," and except if their conditions coordinate with flawlessness (and it once in a while does), they retreat into positive musings, supposing they will give a superior world to everybody with positive articulations.

Some positive masterminds have a heavenly sounding type of forswearing.

"To concentrate on the positive isn't to slight certain notice sign of a "negative" sort that, whenever disregarded, in the end, lead to burden, best case scenario, and catastrophe even from a pessimistic standpoint. When we utilize these negative signs to maintain a strategic distance from calamity, at that point, they're not negative all things considered. "

On account of illness, we can recognize the indications of sickness and get familiar with everything we can to defeat that ailment and move towards that objective. Or then again, we can start by saying that "we have" that infection. In the wake of asserting it as our own long enough, our mind will in general trust it, and our body might be less inclined to dispose of it.

We are advised to live at the time. However, a large portion of us is thinking about the past and additionally the future a large part of the day, so when we will do this, at any rate, make it beautiful.

Keep it adjusted! Contrary reasoning makes everything dreary and terrible. Positive thinking envisions anything, whether practical or not, regardless of whether it's identified with the occasion or not. A few people do this by citing superb (irrelevant) Scriptures whenever someone specifies a pessimistic event.

Concentrate on the positive! That is not positive reasoning!

There is a period for misery and understanding the present actualities. It's about how you manage it. Assuming that you don't accomplish something great isn't contrary reasoning. It's assessing life and how to improve it for yourself.

To cite the above book once more: "Positive reasoning just puts a hole between where you are physically and where you figure you "should" be. There are no "should" to a dangerous disease. You'll be more joyful and likely recuperate quicker, if you let go of the same number of should as you can... It took a ton of contrary reasoning - decades now and again - to expedite a sickness. For what reason should up to 14 days of positive thinking dispose of it?"

Compromise with intelligence somewhere close to the sewer and the mists. Concentrate on the positive, however, make it genuine. Your mind and body know the distinction. Health doesn't come without accepting what you think and state. Your account won't trust the amazing.

DEALING WITH NEGATIVE THOUGHTS

We, as a whole, have negative considerations on occasion. This is typical. For the individuals who experience the ill effects of specific anxiety disorders, contrary reasoning can prompt the beginning of anxiety assaults. When these assaults happen, the individual's satisfaction endures significantly.

The issue with anxiety disorders and contrary reasoning is that one negative idea will regularly form into a progression of all the more dominant negative contemplations. These musings are frequently founded on self-analysis and can lead the individual to trust that the individual in question is by one way or another, not precisely other individuals.

Contrary reasoning, can be controlled once the individual learns a couple of systems. Once leveled out, the individual can start to carry on with an ordinary life once more.

A part of the habits where that you can manage contrary reasoning, which thus can change your conduct, incorporate utilizing strategy known as care.

This is an ancient technique that shows the individual to concentrate on his or her environment and sentiments without being judgmental about either. With this system, there is no set-in stone, fortunate or unfortunate, positive or negative. Things are just what they are, and that's it.

The individual figures out how to stay away from contrary reasoning so that it likewise quiets the nerves and anticipate fits of anxiety. Rather than centering of what is troubling you, you focus on nonpartisan or positive considerations concerning the issue.

The goal behind this strategy isn't to permit the event of negative musings which, as we probably are aware, feed into increasingly negative considerations. By ceasing the cycle from the get-go, you can limit or wipe out anxiety manifestations. It likewise shows you how to abstain from deciding for yourself too cruelly when such judgment isn't justified.

You may likewise profit by utilizing confirmations. These are sure explanations that you rehash to yourself a few times for the day. These positive explanations are particularly valuable when negative idea examples are a danger. Your certifications can be altered to fit any need, whenever.

Both of these strategies enable you to recover control of your manner of thinking. You don't need to endure contrary reasoning if you don't wish it. The key is to supplant negative contemplations with positive considerations.

At whatever point you end up speculation negative contemplations, battle back with positive considerations or attestations. These rehashed positive musings or words will help change your point of view toward the circumstance you are in. You can even keep a diary of your contemplations and scribble down which attestations worked best for a specific issue.

Both of these strategies require practice and will take

some an opportunity to ace. In any case, since they are so incredible and compelling, they merit the speculation. They can enable you to carry on with a more joyful life.

You can see an abundance of data on both of these systems either on the web or disconnected. It is your life, take control of it today.

Step by step instructions to Cope with Anxiety Disorders - Harnessing the Power of the Mind.

What goes on in your mind impacts how you see and identify with yourself and your general surroundings? Put at the end of the day: What you believe is the thing that you feel and carry on. A lot of research has built up that if you are colonized by contrary reasoning; at that point, this might be reflected in low confidence, anxiety disorders, and wretchedness. The causal impact of contrary thinking is robust to the point that anxiety disorders have been marked by individual scientists as 'mistakes in learning.'

Furthermore, the connection between contrary reasoning and anxiety disorders may take a very long time to advance. For instance, there are numerous individuals out there who experience the ill effects of anxiety disorders because of the maltreatment they encounter as kids. Such abuse undermined their feeling of self-esteem; denied them of their certainty and caused in them the inclination to question everything and everyone.

There is a broad scope of negative or distorted contemplations that anxiety issue sufferers battle with. A first fundamental advance in your endeavor to adapt to anxiety disorders is to investigate your reasoning and attempt and recognize your negative considerations. The following are a couple of kinds of negative contemplations that individuals with anxiety disorders may battle with.

The dread of objection: People with an intemperate terror of being disliked by others become excessively touchy to analysis. Their satisfaction lays on the significant conclusions of others. They firmly want to keep others upbeat. They may think that it is hard to disapprove the requests of others. Their own needs turned out to be optional to the need to win the endorsement.

Mental sifting: This happens when an individual tends to harp and ruminate on small negative parts of even the best circumstance and utilize such pessimism to pass unfriendly judgment on oneself. For instance, after a prospective employee meeting, one may stress that he failed to meet expectations since he didn't address one of the inquiries agreeable to him. This might be regardless of the way that the question was not so significant contrasted with the nine others that he addressed skillfully. The individual may then start to see himself as a washout as a result of that one inquiry.

Mind perusing: This is a case whereby you make decisions about what other individuals are thinking with no proof. For instance, you may infer that someone doesn't care for you or he supposes he is superior to you. Mind perusers can have relationship issues since they turned out to be excessively suspicious and doubtful of others.

Over-speculation: Here, one mistake is seen as an example of blunders or errors. For instance, after pounding his vehicle in a mishap, the negative individual may reason that he never does anything appropriately and is a terrible driver.

The entire thought of distinguishing negative musings that influence you as anxiety disorders sufferers is with the goal that you can battle and be free of them. Intellectual Behavioral Therapy gives a well-ordered guide on how to fight contrary reasoning and take out anxiety disorders. On my webpage, you will see, on for all intents and purposes each page, connections to online usual treatment suppliers. The vast majority of these treatments depend on humane cognitive treatment. Intellectual conduct treatment treats anxiety disorders more viable than medications.

How to Make Important Decisions Today

When it comes to making these important decisions without delay, there are a few strategies that may help you out. Many of us are so swamped with work and other stressors in our life that we often fail to realize how easy it often is to simplify more complex situations and processes, in order to make an important decision.

One of the most crucial factors regarding such a decision is that you take a few minutes of quiet time to yourself. Even if you can quickly squeeze in about five minutes. You need to clear your mind of everything, let go of all the clutter. By now, I have already introduced you to a large number of effective strategies that should help you reduce the cluttering in your mind, so it should be easier for you to think more clearly in your quiet time.

Decisions always have an impact on something, but the impact is not always at the same level. Sometimes, a decision may affect how you feel, such as when you decide not to pack lunch for the day. Often, such a small decision would not have a major impact on your life – you can go to the cafeteria and buy something to eat when you feel hungry or during your lunch hour.

Other times, however, decisions have a much larger impact – such as when you have to make a choice that could mean a client would sign a contract with your firm or rather go to another firm. This can be a major loss, especially when the client would be worth millions to your company, should you make the wrong choice and the client goes with their second choice.

The more of an impact a decision will have, the more you would have to consider the different options and ensure that the one you choose will have a most positive impact on your life or your career, compared to the other options that are available to choose from.

Know Your Goals

Prior to making a decision that will have an impact on your life or your career, such as those that may result in a hire from a client, it is vital that you completely understand the goals that you are trying to reach with the particular decision that hangs on your shoulders. Understand exactly what needs to be done with that decision.

For example, is your goal to buy a new house? Understand the smaller goals involved as well. When you are trying to buy a house, you want to ensure there is adequate room for your family, so your goal will be to buy a house that has enough rooms, as well as living space, to accommodate everyone. You also have the goal of choosing a house that is close to schools and to your workplace and that of your wife.

At work, you might need to make a decision on a specific client as there is a conflict between two that you can sign. While the primary goal would be to make money through signing one of these clients, another goal may be to sign the one that could provide your business with a longer-term relationship and projects that will last for several years, even if it means a slightly lower profit on the first project compared to the other client.

As you can see, when you understand what the end goals are – all of them, not just the bigger picture – it becomes much easier to make the right decision.

Be Prepared and Well-Informed

You should be well-informed and very much prepared in order to make a decision that will be best for you, your family, or your business, depending on which party the decision will have an effect on. Thus, always ensure that you obtain as much information as possible related to a project, or whatever it is that is involved before you decide on which option you choose.

If you are going to be buying a house for you and your family, be sure to get information on available properties in your desired area from multiple real estate agencies. Also, make sure that you get as much information as possible on each of the available houses. How many rooms are there? How many bathrooms are there? Does the house have a study? Will you be able to park your car in a garage safely? How safe is the neighborhood? How much should you expect to pay monthly on the mortgage?

The same goes for a business-related decision. Have interviews with the clients that will be affected by your decision. Ask the right questions. Know what they expect. Know what needs to be done. Understand what is involved.

All this information will help you filter out the bad options and choose the option that is best suited for the current scenario.

Make A Biased Decision

It is okay to listen to that gut feeling you get sometimes and to hear out the opinions of other people in your life, whether colleagues, family members, or friends, but it is also important that the decision you made is biased. Even though many would advise being unbiased, I personally find that making decisions in favor of something or someone, such as the parties involved in the situation, really is the best way to go about a decision-making process, and ultimately to avoid constantly finding yourself making delay after delay.

Consider the parties involved and understand what would be considered in their favor when making the final decision. Perhaps your family prefers a dog, so opt for a house with a big yard as compared to a smaller yard or an apartment in a more convenient location – that would be a biased decision based on the preferences of your family.

Weigh Out All the Pros and Cons

Each of the options that you can choose from when you make an important decision has pros and cons involved. It might not always be easy to identify all of the pros and all of the potential drawbacks related to a particular option, but setting up a list of what you know would happen, how you, your family, or perhaps your business could benefit, and what the downsides will be, can be a big help and will ensure making that decision becomes much easier in the end.

Make a list with all the options that are available. Then, set up a sub-list beneath each one. Write down some of the pros and then write down a couple of cons. Be realistic when you write down these factors. Consider all the research that has been done, the information you have gathered, and take the other points I have covered here into account as well.

When you look back at the list you made, you will start to get a better picture of which decision or option is the better choice to make, when comparing the pros and cons of each option in front of you.

Understand Possible Consequences and Complications

Actions have consequences. Sometimes, even making the right decision in life can pose a threat to someone or to some party, and possibly lead to a series of complications. This is why making a list of pros and cons that can be associated with each option you are facing is often not enough. Additionally, you need to consider the chain of reactions that may occur once you make the decision – you need to do this for each of the options that you have listed.

If you choose a house with a bigger yard instead of an apartment in town, then you might have to drive a long way to drop off the kids at school and to get to the office. The reaction here would be the longer distance, which means a longer driving time in the morning and in the afternoon. In turn, you will have to get up earlier and perhaps move faster in the morning. This will also push up your monthly expenses for gas. Your car may need more regular services if you are going to be driving longer distances.

The same type of thought should go into decisions that will affect your career and the company you work at, whether you own the company or simply serve as an employee. If you are going to sign one client over another client, due to a conflict of interest or another related matter, then you need to consider possible consequences that may arise when you choose one particular client. If you need to select a venue, consider possible complications that may arise with each of the options.

Time for Action

After you have done thorough planning, you know the pros and cons of every option in front of you, and you should have an idea of the decision you need to make. Things should be much simpler now and give you the opportunity to make the decision without further delay.

When it is time for action, make the decision. Don't delay again. You have all the information and data that you now need to make the right decision and choose the option that will be most suited to the current situation. Take action, make the decision, and follow the appropriate procedures in order to follow through on that particular decision that you have decided to make.

Following Up on Your Action

This is a step that people usually overlook and, while it is not really a necessity, I highly suggest that you take a moment to reflect on those decisions that you have made. Consider how they have worked out. I personally take 20 minutes once a week in order to follow up on the decisions that I have made during the week. I do this on the weekend when things are calmer. I sit down and take a look at all my notes related to any important decisions that I made. I consider the options I had, and how the one that I ended up choosing affected the particulars and parties involved.

This way, you will be able to learn from your own mistakes and motivate yourself through those decisions that worked out perfectly. Congratulate yourself on successful choices. Don't scold yourself on those that didn't work out great – rather look at why they didn't work out and see what you could have done differently. This way, you can avoid making such mistakes again in the future.

When Is It Better to Delay a Decision?

I know I just gave you the old speech of never delaying a decision and to stop procrastinating, but I do want to touch a quick topic – sometimes, in rare cases, it might be better to delay the process of choosing between different options. It is, however, essential that you understand that this only accounts for special cases and the fact that I am suggesting a possible delay should not give you the opportunity to make excuses when your case does not meet the criteria I am going to discuss here.

First of all, if the decision that you have to make is small and will have no significant impact on your life or in the workplace, then don't delay. No matter how small, the fact that you still need to make that decision will linger in your mind and add to the clutter that may already be present.

For small decisions, consider your options, weigh the pros and cons of each option, and then decide.

When the decision you have to make will have a bigger impact, however, then there are cases where you might want to consider a small delay. At the same time, I want to stress the fact that delaying should not lead to further delaying! One single delay and then, when the time comes, you need to make a choice.

The only time when important decisions should really be delayed is in cases where you feel sick or very tired. For example, if you have caught the flu or you have stayed up all night working on a project. Such scenarios call for rest and healing. ONLY delay the decision up to the time when you have gotten some sleep or when the flu has passed, then immediately start to work on a plan-of-action to ensure you can choose the most appropriate option.

It is usually also advised not to make important decisions when you are upset or angry, as a lot of people find that their emotions get in their way of making informed and realistic decisions. Also, if you feel hungry, try to grab a bite and wait about 20 minutes before you make a final choice.

If you feel especially stressed, try to meditate or do something else that will help you calm down, reduce anxiety, and eliminate stress, then work on making the perfect decision to ensure your project will surely succeed.

Conclusion

You need to train yourself to stop overthinking and make a conscious effort to practice this daily for it to become a habit. Controlling your feelings and thoughts requires serious practice and commitment. If you "Think" about it, this is the only thing we really control 100%, our thoughts and actions. Everything in life comes down to your habits, and every habit started with a thought and then action. SO simply do the same thing to change your habits now.

On its own, your thoughts can drift randomly from one idea to another, it can go down memory lane, chase wild thoughts, or stir up bitter ideas or resentment and anger. Alternatively, your mind can dive into a sea of daydreaming and a world of fantasy, if care is not taken, your life can be controlled by such random thoughts such that every decision or action you take becomes unpredictable. Such intrusive thoughts you might experience during the day is evidence that most of the functions of the mind are likely beyond conscious control. In addition, our thoughts can feel so powerful and real and it can affect the way we perceive the outside world.

Take a moment to discard the assumption that your spontaneous thoughts are meaningless and totally harmless. In truth, such thoughts may be meaningless at that moment, they can be the product of past memory or emotion but in the present moment, they might not reflect reality.

Most of our thoughts are under the control of our subconscious mind and our subconscious mind will never grant us total control over our thoughts. However, you still have the capacity to control some of your thoughts. Also, you can change some of your habits and how you react to them to gain more control over your emotions.

Making conscious efforts to avoid overthinking is a rewarding course of action which will impact the quality of your life significantly. By spending less time going through intrusive, negative thoughts "in your mind" you will have more time to enjoy the present moment and every other moment.

www.ingramcontent.com/pod-product-compliance
Lightning Source LLC
Chambersburg PA
CBHW081349080526
44588CB00016B/2434